ACCELERATED INNOVATION

How Any Business Can Rapidly Innovate to Create an Unfair Advantage

PAUL PRIOR

The author of this book does not dispense medical advice or prescribe the use of any technique as a form of treatment for medical, emotional, or physical problems without the advice of a medical professional, either directly or indirectly. The intent of the author is to offer information in your quest in personal development. In the event you use any of the information in this book for yourself, which is your constitutional right, the author and publisher assume no responsibility for your actions.

Visit the Official Website at:

Printed in the United States of America

First Printing: January 2020

[GRY MTTR]

ISBN: 978-1-5136-5702-8

[GRY MTTR] books may be purchased for educational, business or sales promotional use. Special discounts are available on quantity purchases. For more information, please call or write.

Telephone (353) (0)87-9665296; Email: info@grymttr.org

For orders by U.S. trade bookstores and wholesalers, requests for consultation or speaking engagements, please contact [Paul Prior] at the phone or email address listed above.

For Lorna, Bodhi and Bonnie.
You are nature's masterpiece;
I am merely a spectator in the gallery.

DISCLAIMER

The Author and Publisher has strived to be as accurate and complete as possible in the creation of this book. This book is not intended for use as a source of business, marketing or financial advice. All readers are advised to seek services of competent professionals in the marketing and business fields. Readers are cautioned to rely on their own judgment about their individual circumstances to act accordingly.

While all attempts have been made to verify information provided in this publication, the Publisher assumes no responsibility for errors, omissions, or contrary interpretation of the subject matter herein. Any perceived slights of specific persons, peoples, or organizations are unintentional. This book details the author's own personal experiences and opinions.

The author and publisher are providing this book and its contents on an "as is" basis and make no representations or warranties of any kind with respect to this book or its contents. The author and publisher disclaim all such representations and warranties, including for example warranties of merchantability and educational or medical advice for a particular purpose.

In addition, the author and publisher do not represent or warrant that the information accessible via this book is accurate, complete or current.

Except as specifically stated in this book, neither the author or publisher, nor any authors, contributors, or other representatives will be liable for damages arising out of or in connection with the use of this book. This is a comprehensive limitation of liability that applies to all damages of any kind, including (without limitation) compensatory; direct, indirect or direct, indirect or consequential damages; loss of data, income or profit; loss of or damage to property and claims of third parties.

You understand that this book is not intended as a substitute for consultation with a licensed professional. This book provides content related to educational, marketing and business related topics. As such, use of this book implies your acceptance of this disclaimer.

Table of Contents

Innovation as a competitive advantage

"All change in the world comes from a level of discomfort."

- Barack Obama

There are 1.9 billion Google search results on starting a business and a mere 649 million on how to maintain that success. Given that the average CEO's tenure is five years, we can hazard a guess as to why only 50 of the Fortune Global 500 companies from 1955 still exist today. The sands, however, are shifting as key companies like Apple, Amazon and JP Morgan continue to move towards socially responsible positions and adding value. Like many, I firmly believe that an organisation's existence is directly related to its ability to innovate.

I know what I *should* say. I *should* say that if you are reading this, you have probably shown some success in innovation and are reading outside of your niche, or you are a hobbyist with more than an active interest in innovation. What I *will* say, though, is that if you are reading this, it is highly likely that your innovation efforts are failing. Let us call these instances 'learnings' from now on, shall we?

Well, let me tell you, you are not alone. In fact, you are in the majority (myself included!). Once they reach a certain size - 300 employees and above, if you're wondering - most organisations find it incredibly difficult to innovate. They're like immune systems, waiting to kill a foreign pathogen. Indeed, most of our innovations die well before we know if they can 'cure the disease'.

What makes successful companies continue to be successful? After nearly two decades of trying to answer that, and innovating across dozens of organisations' cultures, I think I can say from experience that there has to be a better way!

You will have to make up your own mind whether you agree with some or all of my remedies. Indeed, you may violently disagree. I look forward to hearing your views, but in the meantime, I genuinely believe only two questions are worth asking:

1. If innovation isn't working for you, what's the reason?

2. What can you do about it tomorrow?

I hope that in the course of this book, you'll find the answers to both.

The three levels of innovation activity

If you are an enterprise-size organisation with a legacy of 'transformation' and own a change budget, you are probably involved in three types of activity, all of which have an innovation aspect:

1. You are fixing stuff.
2. You are future-proofing stuff; and, if you're smart,
3. You are attempting to find the next big thing.

You'll put 80% of your efforts into fixing and future-proofing and the remaining 20% into finding the next big thing. So, why don't we start with the 80%?

You are fixing stuff

It's only natural that you'll spend about 50% of your time on ensuring your organisation continues to operate soundly. This could mean SAP/Oracle/'insert big technology platform here' upgrades, undertaking lean projects to remove organisational waste, moving staff to low-cost locations, in-sourcing or outsourcing options or manipulating one of the thousands of Excel sheets that underpin a business. If you imagine a US apartment block, this is like the landlord and janitor combined: the janitor maintains the status quo and ensures everything is working correctly, while the landlord ensures everything that is working is also making money.

You are future-proofing stuff

By now, most of you are at least evaluating the 'start-up' ecosystem for potential partners, quite rightly. You get the benefit of accelerated and flexible technologies, while they get the benefits of decades of experience and a ready-made data set. (Not all of these companies are start-ups, incidentally. Many are going concerns, but that would be a book in its own right.)

Most future-proofing appears to be on the basis of what I call imitation theory: "Our competitors are doing it, so we must too." It's like feeling obliged to get your fence painted because your neighbours have. This isn't a bad motivating factor in itself: we all need to be aware of what our competitors are doing. But a horse that spends too much time looking at its rivals will stumble and lose the race.

Innovative future-proofing technology includes process mining and automation, the development of self-service platforms, most Salesforce or CRM implementations, data mining and analytics, customer experience mapping and the creation of 'centres of excellence'. All add value, but are commoditised.

There is a worthy book in either fixing or future-proofing your business. Knowingly or not, plenty of innovation approaches concentrate on both. But that's boring. Let's get down to brass tacks and talk about your search for the next big thing.

The next big thing

A company's ability to sustain multiple successes is directly proportional to its ability to build its customer base while at least maintaining margin. You may want to attract business from a new cohort, or to pre-empt the market by developing your next phase of products and services. If you are, you're devoting about 20% of your time and resources to thinking about the next big thing. I'd imagine you also have a certain level of tolerance when it comes to failure: somewhere between one out of five and one out of eight. The truth is, if you're really pushing the boundaries, it's more like one in ten or one in 20. My objective is to enable you to identify the next big thing while vastly increasing your chances of doing so. Quite a tall order, I know!

But before we do that, let's talk about what might not be working for you.

Why innovation may not be working for you today

"Wrong does not cease to be wrong because the majority share in it."

– Leo Tolstoy

I once attended a seminar by Tony Robbins, the motivational speaker and self-improvement evangelist who travels the world helping people believe in themselves. After one day listening to this guy, I felt empowered, motivated, energetic and confident in anything I wanted to pursue. I could have lifted a car in that moment. Unfortunately, two weeks later, I was back in my Harry Potter pyjamas, drinking herbal tea and complaining about the dishwasher.

Is this really any different to spending an afternoon sticking Post-it Notes on a wall, consumed by the sheer number of Post-its, the intensity of the session and the sensation of sweaty armpits? You certainly walk out feeling empowered, motivated, energetic and confident in anything the organisation wants to pursue; yet two weeks later, you're consumed with objections, back on the hamster wheel, bemoaning the methodology (or the facilitators) and overwhelmed by the need to firefight.

Look, there is nothing wrong with feeling empowered, motivated, energetic and confident. I wrote a large cheque to Tony in order to do so. Nevertheless, there is everything wrong with giving your valuable time to something that does not achieve a step change in business performance.

However, before we get into the whys, whats and hows, it's worthwhile talking about methodology. There are as many fads in innovation as there are posts on Kim Kardashian's Instagram account. None are useless, all have strengths and weaknesses, and most are never deployed in the corporate world the way they were intended. Let's spend some time discussing these.

Agile

What is it?

Popularised by the Agile Manifesto in 2001, what started as nine Agile methodologies has been repackaged as SCRUM, a well-defined sequence of practices for iterative releases. A more recent permutation, the Scaled Agile

Framework, looks to overcome Agile's inability to work at scale and has grown in popularity with enterprise-size software houses. Today, the word Agile is used in broad terms to describe a company whose structure is flexible in adapting to both the market and its own culture.

Why is it?

Organisations are obsessed with the concept of flexibility since the rise of emergent strategy and disruptive technologies. On paper, Agile provided a robust framework that allowed organisations to achieve this, particularly in the area of software development. It has since been broadened to define agility at an organisational level.

What it is not

An innovation framework for the deployment of new products and services. Agile is a way of working, supported by a number of well-defined practices. It does not require its impact to be quantified.

How companies actually deploy it

The vast majority of organisations that think about Agile deploy Kanban boards, a visual management technique to limit work in progress. In the end, they look more like a Jackson Pollock painting: in their quest to be Agile, they only become more chaotic. Nothing epitomises this more than SCRUM meetings that are meant to take 15 minutes but end up lasting 90.

A well-known example of an Agile organisation is General Electric. One of its performance management innovations, the PD@GE app, enables each employee to set objectives and obtain real-time feedback. The premise is to focus on transparency, honesty and continuous improvement.

Design Thinking

What is it?

American professor John E. Arnold was one of the first to consider Design Thinking back in the 1950s, but it wasn't until 2011 that Michael Plattner kicked off the innovation angle. Following this, companies like IDEO and Google popularised it. Design Thinking consists of five stages: Empathise, Defining the Problem, Ideation, Prototyping and Validating.

Empathise

Empathy, defined as "the ability to understand and share the feelings of others", is an important part of Design Thinking. It's important that experts observe, immerse themselves and put themselves in the shoes of those who are involved in the day-to-day problem you're looking to solve. This is the essence of human-centred design: to gain insights by setting aside our own biases and assumptions.

Defining the Problem

Based on the observations made, we analyse behaviour to determine the core problems. The resulting problem statement is written in a way that relates to human beings. For instance: "Individuals over the age of 70 want to work so they feel they still have a contribution to make to society."

This statement is then extended to include features, functions and other useful elements. It's useful to proceed to the next stage with a comment such as: "How might we… help individuals over the age of 70 who want to work?"

Ideation

Having observed behaviour and formulated a problem statement, we can now begin generating ideas. Using techniques such as reverse problem definitions, SCAMPER and brainstorming, the aim of Ideation is to look at the problem in a totally new way: to 'think outside the box'.

Prototyping

Based on the Ideation session, we now produce a number of inexpensive minimal viable products. If it's a digital design, wireframe tools such an InVision, Moqups or Balsamiq allow you to collaborate and share the prototype, generating instant feedback. This is an experimental phase, designed to iterate through a number of solutions in a short timeframe.

Validating

With a digital product, this is where you bring in User Experience, Customer Experience and IT to rigorously test the wireframe you have designed. What you're looking to ascertain in this final phase is how close the finished product is to what the intended users expect.

There are also five golden rules to Design Thinking.

Design Thinking should remain social

It is vital that Design Thinking be 'human-centric'.

We must preserve ambiguity

Innovation demands experimentation, so we need to enter into Design Thinking with the requisite freedom of thought to ensure its success.

All Design is redesign

Design Thinking asserts that it is important to look at how problems have been solved historically to understand where they are going in the future.

Prototypes = Communication

It is a misconception to view prototyping as a design mechanism. In fact, it is a communication mechanism.

The largest manufacturer of Post-it Notes, 3M, has seen its share price surge since 2011. That should give you all the insight you need on Design Thinking.

Why is it?

As organisations became more 'project-centric', they also became incredibly time-poor. Design Thinking allowed for short, efficient bursts of creativity (ideation) using a structure that is easy to understand and implement. The process defines problems in an intuitive way and understanding its application does not require a large investment of time. It is also relatively self-contained and does not push organisations too far out of their comfort zones, benefiting those that find it difficult to transform.

What it is not

Design Thinking's biggest critics poor cold water on the level of simplification, and the fact that it lends itself well to validation using purely anecdotal means. It is also highly subjective to bias. Design Thinking does create space for iterative ideation, but it does not take responsibility for the success of what has been ideated.

How companies actually deploy it

Design Thinking can be useful in defining customer experiences or iterative product improvements in a well-defined customer grouping (e.g. high earners for a bank or schoolkids for a bookshop). It is therefore appropriate to 'I want to fix' and to an extent 'I want to future-proof' innovations. That's assuming it's in the right hands: many of the organisations I visit have diluted it down to at best a teambuilding exercise with some ideation.

There is a famous story of Airbnb facing bankruptcy in 2009. The founders, along with entrepreneur Paul Graham of Y Combinator, evaluated 40 of their adverts in New York and realised that the photography was inconsistent to the point that it was very difficult to determine the quality of the holding. They set themselves the simple task of developing a solution, using the talents of designer Joe Gebbia, who had studied Design Thinking.

Acorns is a financial services and financial technologies company, founded in 2014, which employs over 350 people and has more than 3.7 million users. Its accessible trading application, to empower the average person to invest their spare change, includes features such as a debit card, instant saving and spend strategies. In fact, its strong user experience reflects the essence of Design Thinking. As vice-president David Keegan puts it: "At Acorns, we try to build experiences that really convey a story to users. We think a lot about the psychology behind how people think about money, and the personal narratives everyone has about where they are in their finances now and where they want to be." Genius!

Figure 1: Taken from https://www.acorns.com/

Lean Innovation

What is it?

Combining elements of Agile, Design Thinking and Lean Startup, Lean Innovation continues the trend of adding the word 'lean' to emphasise efficiency. It is built on the principles of empathy, experiments and evidence. We've talked already about Agile and Design Thinking. The next concept, Lean Startup - established by author and entrepreneur Eric Ries in 2011 - is built on five principles.

1. You don't have to work in a garage to be an entrepreneur.
2. A new kind of management is required for a startup.

3. Startups exist to learn how to build a sustainable business.
4. We need to focus on the boring stuff (e.g. a new accounting mechanism for startups).
5. It's important to build-measure-learn.

Lean Innovation focuses on waste in innovation such as defining a market that is too broad, developing functionality that a customer does not need, not sharing information, testing without learning or thinking in silos. It encompasses three sets of activities: doing the right thing, doing it right and getting better.

At its core are seven elements:

Gemba

Gemba stands for the place in which "truth can be found". It emphasises the need to experience the problem you're solving in real life before determining how it should be solved.

Front loading

Front loading, a term that originates in project management, is the allocation of resourcing at the start of a process. This is in contrast to allocating resourcing evenly across the course of a process. It also speaks to decision-making, holding decisions in a parking lot to a future date.

Visual management

This involves using visual techniques to display information and includes the description of a solution, a list of decisions, action plans and a progress chart.

Timeboxing

Timeboxing means allocating a specific period to a specific set of deliverables. Typically, the deliverable is broken down in such a way as to be consistent with others in the timebox. It is also judged to be possible in the timeframe.

One-Piece Flow

Numerous studies have found that multitasking is not the optimal way to manage your time. In our working lives, we are constantly managing competing priorities in a fragmented way. Lean Innovation recommends concentrating on one-piece flow - in other words, doing one thing at a time.

Heartbeat

Organisations, like living organisms, have a heartbeat, a rhythm of how things are done. Innovation is no different: the rhythm is encapsulated by a pipeline or launch plan for the new product or service, designed to minimise any adverse impact and maintain motivation.

Prototyping

Prototyping is the common element across all innovation methodologies and its utilisation has increased by 300% in the past decade. It means using an accelerated method to design a new product or service, on paper format or using digital tools such as Moqups, InVision or Azure.

Why is it?

Unlike those corporate organisations that remain stuck in structures established at the time of Taylorism, Lean Innovation recognises that modern organisations require a new structure and looks to encompass 12 different principles across four pillars.

- Strategy and performance
    - Customer value
    - Strategy & leadership Commitment
    - Track performance
- Skilled people and collaboration
    - Human skills
    - Chief engineer
    - Cross-functional collaboration
- Efficient process
    - Co-create, share and reuse knowledge

  - o Lean Thinking tools & methods
  - o Sustainable innovation
- Continuous improvement
  - o Communicate, manage and reward change
  - o Internal and external partnerships
  - o Continuous improvement

What it is not

Lean Innovation is comprehensive in its ability to combine the strategic, continuous improvement, collaboration and strategic aspects of good governance. It requires an organisation to truly invest in its success across multiple areas of the business, which can be a lot to take on. It is, however, limited in methodology to allow you to better understand the marketplace, increase wallet share in new customer areas or monitor outcomes for differentiated product and service design.

How companies actually deploy it

As most organisations search for cheaper, faster alternatives, and due to the relative 'newness' of lean innovation, organisational adoption has been slow. The alignment between strategy and execution can be tenuous at times, leading to a lack of cascaded accountability. Cross-functional collaboration, continuous improvement and the implementation of lean thinking have been popularised by the likes of Shopify. Meanwhile the idea of rewarding change, which should be taken seriously, seldom makes it past a statement of work. Much like Agile, we will see a decoupling of Lean Innovation and adoption of some of its parts.

A company that has seen some success using the Lean Startup elements of Lean Innovation is Votizen, which launched in 2007 to organise US voters online. Founder David Binetti used A/B testing product features (using two versions of a webpage or app to determine which performs better), messaging and design to increase the ease of us. His methods produced significant improvements, including a 13% increase in registration rates and an activation rate of over 90%.

Open Innovation

What is it?

Popularised by Henry Chesbrough, Open Innovation concentrates on the 'outside in' to bring external ideas and technologies into internal innovation practices. The type of business model your organisation deploys dictates the type of collaboration and the technique is notable for partnerships with academic institutions. One example is the Netflix Prize, which sought to improve the now-famous recommendation engine by 10% with the help of external ideas.

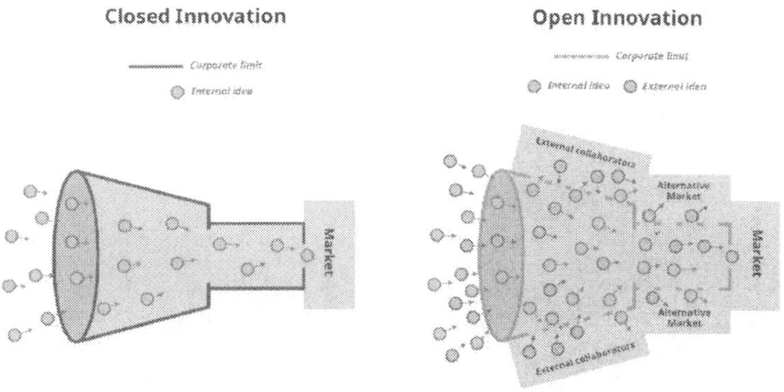

Figure 2: Taken from https://www.viima.com/blog/open-innovation.

Why is it?

Open Innovation embraces transparency and is at odds with the more introverted innovation techniques in many regulated entities. It has brought academic collaboration into private corporations and elements have been used to open incumbent organisations to the world of start-ups and going concerns. The principles that underpin it dictate (correctly) that the business model is just as important as the go-to market strategy.

- We must find and elicit knowledge from external sources.
- External R&D will create value, internal R&D will allow us to claim it.
- We do not have to own the research to profit from it.

- Building a better business model trumps first-mover advantage.
- Internal + external ideas = winning.
- We buy IP and profit from use of our own IP.

What it is not

Open Innovation describes what you must do, but is limited in describing how you must do it. It therefore lacks a robust methodology for achieving success through partnerships or a methodology for new product or service design. Moreover, it requires patience and a willingness to embrace failure. It does not guarantee that partnerships will be successful and has been known to be subject to groupthink or crowdthink.

How companies actually deploy it

The continued rise of open source and 'ecosystems' is a form of Open Innovation. By collaborating with Starling Bank - a digital, mobile-only challenger bank - Barclays, one of the UK's largest financial services organisations, gains a new way to frame the problem of customer acquisition and better use of technology for iterative disruption.

FirstBuild, a GE initiative that creates "a socially engaged community focused on the next great idea", was formed with a group of venture capitalists, giving the public an opportunity to contribute to the design of home appliances.

Danish toy brand Lego takes advantage of Open Innovation through the Create and Share and LEGO Ideas websites. In the case of Lego Ideas, the firm evaluates a design when a threshold of 10,000 supporters is reached. One successful launch - a set of mini-figures based on US sitcom *The Big Bang Theory* - took place ten months after the idea was mooted.

In the world of home entertainment, Netflix's recommendation engine is reported to be worth $1 billion a year. This innovation came about after the media services provider, which is 20 years old and employs more than 5,000 people, came up with the $1 million Netflix Prize. The winning team, BellKor's Pragmatic Chaos, met Netflix's challenge, substantially improving the accuracy of predictions about how much someone will enjoy a movie based on their existing preferences. This feeds into the Netflix recommendation engine, increasing the level of choice available to consumers. Genius!

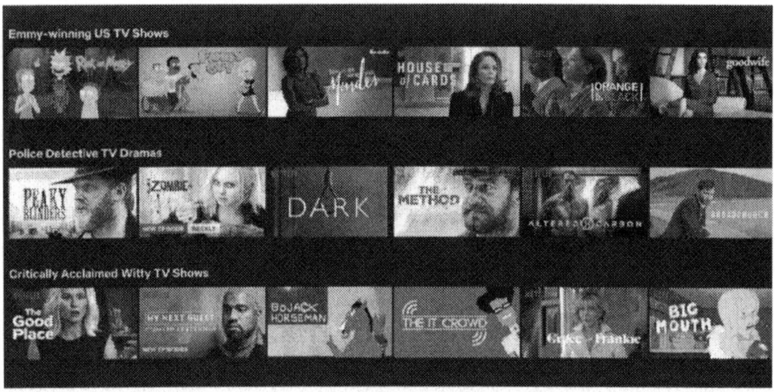

Figure 3: Taken from https://www.topbots.com/netflix-movie-recommender-system-rework/

I'll stop there, as Jan Spruijt has compiled a list of 71 Innovation Methodologies at *openinnovation.eu,* which you can review.

The seven failures

"It takes 20 years to be an overnight success."

- Eddie Cantor

Those of you who have listened to me meander at one of the many conferences I have spoken at in recent years will know that I speak about organisations' seven failings when it comes to approaching innovation. Let's discuss them.

We cannot disrupt ourselves

Many have written about the art of disruption but none moreso than pioneer Clayton Christensen. An incredibly humble man, he speaks in depth about how corporations cannot disrupt themselves - unless, that is, they are courageous enough to set up a completely autonomous innovation unit. This decision tree paves the way.

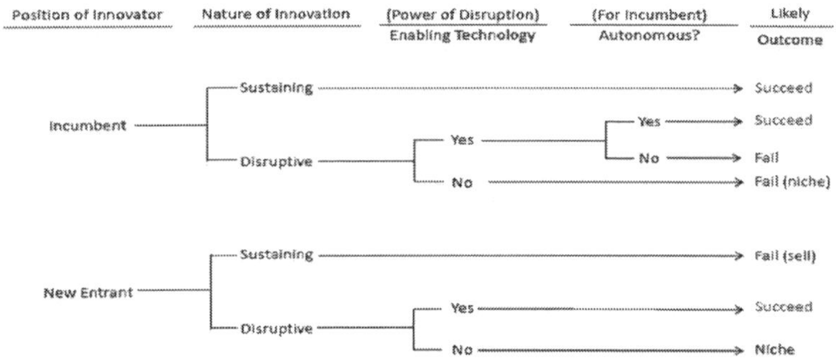

Sustaining technologies are the likes of Robotic Process Automation and Analytics. Disruptions refers to an event that interrupts the normal course or continuation of the nature of service that you provide and may include elements of Blockchain and Instant Payments (Open APIs). It is possible for the next big thing to be delivered through sustaining or disruptive technologies.

We lack patience and resolve

Confucius, a teacher in the 4th century BC, was at one point Chief Justice to the State of Lu in China. Shortly after he took office, a father and a son filed a lawsuit at his court. The father charged his son with disrespect and asked Confucius to bring the son to justice. Separately, the son accused his father of causing him embarrassment. The two kept bickering in court. Confucius, however, did not deliver his verdict right away. It was his right to sentence either party to prison time but instead, he placed them in custody together. After a month, the father asked that the charges be dropped as the two were reconciled.

The point is that sometimes we do not have to do anything. With patience and resolve, a solution will present itself.

Unfortunately, if anything, modern organisational governance has worsened. For many of us who control a budget, our conversations no longer take place in September-October but are monitored quarterly, monthly and even weekly – with projects expected to achieve two to three times return on investment. I am not suggesting it is wrong to be commercially diligent, in fact later I will argue in favour of it. Nevertheless, assumptions underpin innovation, particularly disruptive innovations. By nature they are fluid and cannot conform to traditional budgeting processes, therefore seeing them through requires a certain amount of patience and resolve.

We struggle with objectivity

I worked for a fintech in my 20s and soon found myself in the office of a well-known group CEO – let's call him Brad for the sake of politeness. Up until this point, most of my conversations had been with shopkeepers, my professors or the guy who delivered the post to me; so, needless to say; I was nervous. I remember I must have gone to the bathroom about seven times. This man had three executive assistants; I barely had three shirts.

Luckily, as I sat outside his office, one of his well-meaning executive assistants took pity on me and asked would

I join her for tea in the canteen. I explained that I would be late for my meetings and she told me that she could easily move it by 15 minutes. When I added that my nervousness was based on a perceived lack of experience, she gave me advice that I've spent my career trying to implement. She told me I was lucky. "Most people bring with them a lifetime's worth of baggage. You bring with you wonder and naivety, and it's rare to be presented with that level of objectivity."

I've often reflected on this conversation, and my interpretation is that human beings are sh*t at objectivity. We bring baggage that informs our perceptions and leads to distrust, we think everyone is trying to sell to us and as a result, we rarely truly engage in what can be the right solutions for our organisation.

Snapchat, a multimedia messaging app that launched in 2011, has more than 2,700 staff. It focused on the permanency of messages and pictures to create a new application for people who wanted privacy (its messages become inaccessible after a short time). The subjective approach would be to look at Instagram, decide the market was saturated and think that a small iteration would not have significant customer traction. Objectively Snapchat knew better, and was still achieving 8% growth in 2019.

We suffer from organisation myopia

By myopia, I'm talking about our tendency to focus on the company's needs, rather than defining the company in terms of customers' needs and wants.

In 2014, I was privileged to run a Meet the Need workshop for the first time with a financial services organisation. We listened to the feedback the customer representative gave us on products and services and the outcomes customers required from us. A shy but honest contributor called Carol spoke about how she garnered advice about financial investments. She'd hosted a garden party one summer evening, and her niece had attended with a new boyfriend. As inquisitive aunts do, she'd struck up a conversation with the young man, a former investment banker who was building an app that used a chatbot to give financial advice. He'd pulled out his iPhone and shown her how it worked.

As Carol told her story, a project manager on one of our client's transformation workstreams butted in, saying her story was not indicative of "our customers". He added that "most people" want to talk to a financial adviser, so the application would be no use to them.

Once I got over my shock, I remembered the executive assistant's advice from long ago and thought objectively about what I had just witnessed. This person had spent two decades with this institution, had never heard customer feedback directly and was managing a project that was about to go live with a product that bore no relation to what he'd just heard. It was an excellent example of organisational myopia: he simply felt that he and his employer knew what was best for customers. There are times when this is the case, but this wasn't one of them.

We are blind to bias

We speak at a rate of 250 words a minute and think at least ten times as fast, so by the time the words leave our mouth (or are written down) they are already filtered through years of bias. Think of any meeting you have been in that's had about ten participants. In any medium-to-large organisation, you will typically find the following eight types of bias:

Availability cascade: "If I keep repeating it, it will be true."

Verbatim effect: "Yes, yes, I get the gist."

Mere exposure effect: "Hmmm, yes, that sounds familiar."

Courtesy bias: "You're right John, I agree."

Reactance: "I hear what you're saying, but I'm going to do the exact opposite."

Framing effect: "Ah yes, that's exactly what I was thinking!"

Choice-supportive bias: "Yes, that lean project we did was amazing."

Default bias: "Yes, let's just do exactly what you just said."

Your ability to recognise and respond to bias will be a key factor in success in innovation.

We are stuck in the elusion structure

Elusion is the act of successfully hiding or escaping from something, mostly accountability in this case (or in Freudian terms, ourselves). The elusion structure is the unofficial operating model of organisations and how information really flows. I would hope most of us are familiar with *The Simpsons*, so I use the analogy of seven characters to describe the elusion structure below.

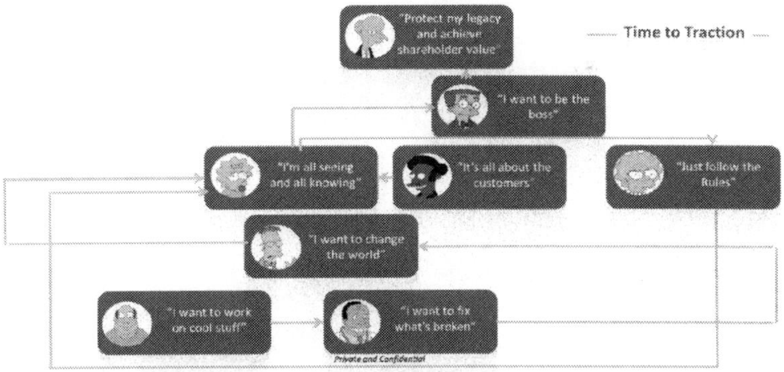

The narrative goes something like this.

"Comic Book Guy just wants to work on cool stuff and identifies Artificial Intelligence as a potential technology innovation that will allow him to do so. Dr Hibbert is on board once he understands how it is going to fix a number of problems within the current processes. Professor Fink is Head of Innovation and wants to change the world, to an extent he is p*ssed off that the recommendation did not come from him, but relents because he feels he is part of the process. He then communicates with Maggie, who is Director of Operations. Maggie has been getting it in the ear from Apu, who is "all about the customers", and wonders how it might affect customers. This results in a conversation with Lisa in Risk and Compliance. Lisa feels the current proposal, which Dr Hibbert, Prof Frink and Comic Book Guy are wedded to, lacks analysis of the legal implications and sends it back to Maggie. Maggie convenes the team and discusses the compromises that need to made. Once agreed, the proposal is sent to Lisa again for sign-off. At the weekly senior management team meeting, chaired by Waylon Smithers, Lisa gives an update on how this technology could innovate various processes under management. Smithers loves the idea and asks for return on investment from Lisa before communicating it to Mr Burns."

I'm exhausted just writing that. Every single organisation I have ever worked with that has grown beyond 300 people has some form of elusion structure in place. Governance is there for good reason, but we must tackle this structure for innovation to take place.

We ignore the systemic needs of people

Many thought leaders write about the need to understand culture, both macro and micro, to assure innovation success. Professor Geert Hofstede, a Dutch social psychologist, has built a career on talking about how cultures differ across regions, countries and companies - in particular, the effect the power-distance relationship has. Developing an innovation method that tackles macro culture seemed like a tall order for me. Therefore, like a good innovator, I started 'sorting for sameness' in trying to understand the psychological [as opposed to Maslow's basic] needs at a very human level. This brought me to self-determination theory, which states at a basic human level, we have three needs:

1. The requirement for a sense of belonging (Relatedness)
2. The requirement for a sense of importance (Competence)
3. The requirement for a sense of freedom of choice (Autonomy)

There can be a fourth, which is the requirement for a sense of benefiting others. In the moral sense, it's useful for innovation as it brings you closer to the end-user. However, I believe this to be highly subjective; there are many successful innovators that do not have this.

Whether the needs amount to three or four, can we all agree that if you want to bypass company and country culture, you have to meet them?

One could argue that all the innovation methods mentioned created a sense of belonging, since most involve bringing groups of people together. They are designed to be collaborative and inclusive, to make you feel warm and fuzzy inside. You may also argue that Design Thinking creates a sense of freedom of choice in that it quickly whittles down ideas in the Ideation phase, but then offers little quantification to balance this choice and ensure the correct commercial decisions are made. I doubt anyone feels an increased sense of importance from any of the methods.

Traditional vs accelerated approach

"The definition of insanity is doing the same things over and over again, and expecting different results."

- NARCOTICS ANONYMOUS.

If you have an innovation centre, you more than likely have an innovation approach that's aligned to your budgeting process, and looks something like this. If you do not recognise this, feel free to skip this section and go straight to the Accelerated Approach section.

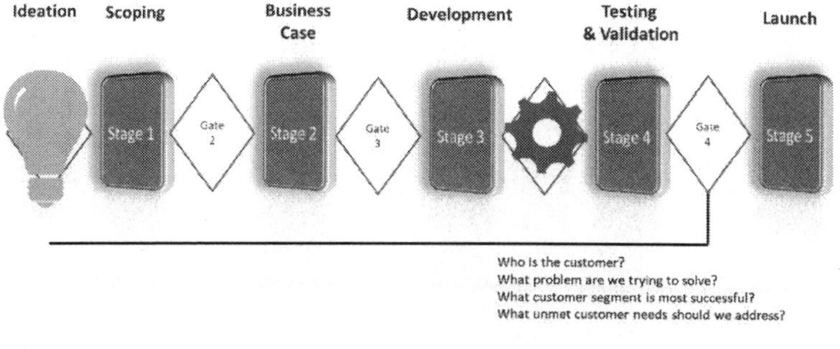

This approach's success is in direct proportion to your confidence in the information at your disposal, and how closely that is aligned to those who intend to use this new product or service. Let's discuss each stage:

Stage 1: Ideation

In 2006, at the height of the Apple iPod, most technology organisations were threatened by the large-scale public uptake of this new device. None more so than Microsoft, who quickly ideated a competitive mobile music device called the Zune, in partnership with Toshiba. This was discontinued in 2011. Why? Because consumers rejected the clunky design and lack of differentiated feature set, and the push was not strong enough to pull consumers from the iPod.

Ideation is defined as "the formation of ideas or concepts". In a sense, it gives organisations free rein in terms of how they choose to ideate. The majority use some form of Design Thinking or Design Sprints, or at least stick a few Post-it Notes on a wall and prioritise them. Most of the time they are restricted by availability and competing priorities, so the pressure is on to make these sessions shorter, which has a knock-on effect in terms of creating an environment for innovation.

Stage 2: Scoping

As soon as the ideation session is over, and one or two core ideas are agreed upon by the group (by which I really mean the Head of Innovation), you need to go 'ask for money'. The 'ask for money' process is the same as any other request for funding: you have to create a statement of work. What are the risks? What are the benefits? What's the resource requirement? What's the scope? Once the scoping activity is complete, it goes into the mix to compete against all the other projects. If you are lucky, the projects committee or your equivalent senior executive signs it off.

For really well-known problems or unmet needs, or innovations in the 'I'm fixing stuff' vein, there is nothing wrong with this approach, other than its cumbersome nature. When it comes to 'I'm future-proofing stuff' or 'attempting to find the next big thing', it is silly to assume we can budget in the same way as everything else. How can one define the scope of something that's based on assumptions turning out to be true? How can one scope when the end-user is not even part of the process?

Stage 3: Business Case

If you have not lost the will to live during the scoping stage, your innovative new product or service will be described in a business case. This includes the trajectory of return on investment, based on assumptions that have more than likely not been validated by those who intend to use the product or service. At this point, you could be months into the process, which means the market for the product or service (assuming it's based on technology) has probably shifted.

Stage 4: Development

Once the Business Case is signed off, anything up to two months later (I saw six months once!), we can be forgiven for feeling excited about bringing the product or service to life. If it is a technology innovation, then we are subject to a release cycle within the organisation (which most of the time follows a linear, sequential 'waterfall' approach). If you are part of a large enterprise, you have to fight for a slot within the release cycle, which might be as rare as once every quarter or half-year! That's if you're thinking in these terms at all.

Smart enterprises have the notion of hybrid (or bimodal), which means the innovative product or service can at least move at a different pace to accommodate technology changes. However, it is still subject to the same level of governance when moving into production.

It is common for this cycle of innovation to come up against processes and capabilities that are not designed to bring it to market. Even the most determined innovators struggle to contain their frustration sometimes.

Stage 5: Validation & Test

Validation & Test can come perhaps eight to ten months after the ideation session. At this point, even if you test with the user group, a great deal of the momentum has all but dissipated and project managers just want to get the job done. In the majority of cases, organisations seem to have a weird nervousness about testing with customers and usually use staff composites, who feel obliged to be relatively positive. No one wants to air their dirty laundry in front of customers, as it were, but as companies like the US technology firm Stripe (and many a research student) has postulated, there is a direct correlation between transparency and trust.

This all leads to two simple perspectives. Firstly, that testing at eight months means you've already incurred significant cost; and secondly, that after eight months, the probability of choice-supportive bias is high. This means that we push the product through, even when feedback indicates that we ought to abandon it. In any event, senior stakeholders who signed off on the project will be reluctant to announce any failure publicly. For mobile devices, this usually leads to a 'soft launch' to a significantly reduced and more favourable customer set.

Stage 6: Launch

Finally, we launch the product or service. Mostly we do so with little communication strategy and take an 'under-the-radar' approach. For non-technology innovations, it's a soft launch at best. This may result in small changes, along with - usually - a significant amount of documentation that sits in a filing cabinet and gathers dust. Technology innovations are a little different. In the case of an 'I want to fix' innovation, you will usually find success as it pertains to a well-understood problem, even though it still took significantly longer than it should have. For an 'I want for the future' innovation, what is released is usually a watered-down version of what was ideated, with little monitoring of benefits. Chances are that the development team and project manager will take a sigh of relief that anything was released at all.

I am being facetious, but ask yourself seriously if this is THAT far from the truth. How many of your innovations have made it to production? And of those, how many achieved the traction you needed to produce benefits, or were freely accepted by the business?

The Great Unveil

"Paul, if you save me $200 million, that's equally as beneficial as making me $200 million."

- A CLIENT.

At the start of my career, I was undertaking induction training for one of the many organisations I have worked with. A very senior member of staff took time out of what must have been a very busy day to meet with me. I was grateful. In the course of the conversation, I was taken through a history of success in the organisation, the types of clients they work with, how successful projects were and how positively the market viewed the brand. None of this was a lie, but the concept of a decades-old organisation that didn't have any failures really bothered me. I plucked up the courage to ask about failures and was subsequently told they had none. Look up this organisation on the internet, however, and you'll find high-profile failures alongside multiple examples of successes.

I understood the point here. The senior member of staff wanted to have a positive conversation and portray the organisation in a good light to a new recruit. But even at that age, I had failed miserably on a number of occasions. Later, as my career matured, I realised that a consultant who saves a client from making a bad decision is just as valuable as one who helps them make a good decision.

This interaction was a springboard for me. I started to think about the role innovation can play in maintaining the success of already successful companies, and an accelerated approach to doing so. So, without further ado, let's start by depicting the five stages of that process.

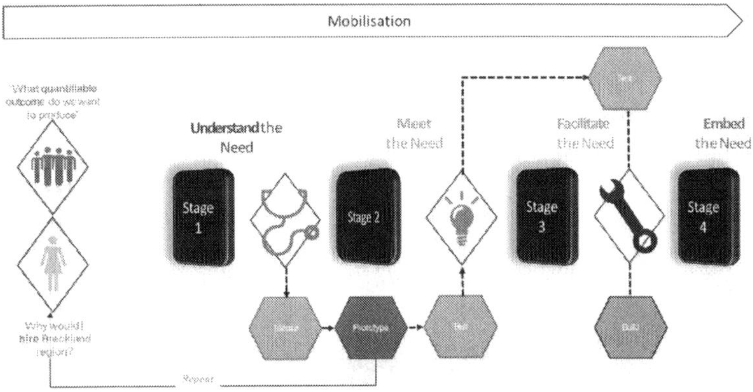

Each stage has a very clear objective, described in the following table. Don't worry if the terms are new to you, we will introduce them later.

	Stage	Objective
0	**Mobilisation**	Objective: to create a space of innovation, select the participants from your organisation who will immerse themselves in the process, and the vertical segments of 'customers' who will inform it.
1	**Understand the Need**	Objective: to bring together the Jobs Canvas, Implicit Journey Map, Interview scripts and Best Practice insights to inform the 50-100 outcomes that have the greatest probability of success.
2	**Meeting the Need**	Objective: to bring together both the vertical segmented 'customers' and staff to co-design the outcomes across a number of succinct elements.
3	**Facilitate the Need**	Objective: to bring together operational staff, the inherent processes of your organisation, representation of the vertical segments and the prioritised co-designed outcomes to bring out any objections and co-design the operationalisation of the preferred outcomes.

4	**Embed the Need**	Objective: to design a number of communication mechanisms that will be used to "spread the message" across the organisation, the completed conversational journey documentation and, finally, the agile requirements that are ready to be implemented by your transformation programme or the BAU change team.

Stage 0: Mobilisation

"Give me six hours to chop down a tree and I will spend the first four sharpening the axe."

- Abraham Lincoln

The greatest journeys start with a single step and the clients I have seen that innovate successfully are those that also mobilise effectively.

Assuming you are an organisation with more than 100 people, we can safely assume you have a configuration of five people that can represent 80% of the tacit knowledge of your business. Identifying these representatives is time well spent.

Where do they come from? Well, one representative will be someone who understands your end customer. 'Customer' is meant in the broadest terms here: it can be a buyer, another business, another department or an employee. Another representative will come from technology, then Risk and Compliance, Operations and finally a senior executive who will sponsor. The sponsor should be on the board or another decision-making authority and is accountable for ensuring the team has the autonomy, budget and decision-making ability to carry through the outcomes. A sixth person would be a facilitator; a seventh would commonly be the facilitator in training (the train-the-trainer approach is the only way with this methodology). Henceforth, this team will be known as the innovation team.

If you are hoping to identify a potential facilitator within your organisation, look for the outliers, the people whom others may identify as 'difficult' or a 'disrupter'. Many a time they are the hotdeskers, naturally curious or quite often those that have tattoos, piercings or an individualistic dress style. I've never met a true innovator who wears a navy dress suit or a black dress suit of their own accord. Have you?

No group will ever "storm" as much as this group will if they are facilitated the right way. It should feel uncomfortable at first, as discomfort is our gut check for knowing we are solving problems and learning in an intrinsically different way. This right way can be encapsulated in three activities.

Firstly, the innovation team need to be trained in how to deal with group situations with customers.

I once worked with a financial services organisation that, for the first time in its 100-year history, appreciated the need to interact with those buying its services in a less biased way (i.e. outside of surveys and feedback). The innovation team had within its ranks a technology role - a project manager called Fred - who had spent eight months attempting to support financial advisers in conversations with potential customers. We were all excited by the Meeting the Need workshop (described next) and a number of senior stakeholders committed the time to attend.

At one point, we were co-designing a solution with a customer and opened up the floor for comments. A 73-year-old woman called Agnes spoke up and mentioned that she had met her niece's boyfriend at a recent family gathering. As she'd been sizing him up, he'd shown her a financial advice app that was big in the US. The app, Acorns, was designed to help unsophisticated investors invest their spare change in the stock market.

She'd been flabbergasted at how intuitive the interface was, convincing her immediately that financial advice received via "the internet" would help her to spend her pension wisely.

When she shared this experience with the group, I could see Fred growing agitated. As soon as she'd made the point that in her view, an in-person conversation with a financial adviser was no longer a requirement, he rudely interrupted.

More than that, he launched into a 17-minute tirade (I counted!) on the benefits of in-person financial advice, directly challenged the truthfulness of what she was saying and closed with the words: "You're wrong." After that, a shaken Agnes barely contributed.

An unfortunate side of being human is that we are biased towards our own opinions. Organisation myopia assures us that we know more about what others want than they know themselves.

It is therefore imperative to run a two-hour lunch and give participants guidance in how to navigate scenarios like this. It's shocking how little we listen, let alone listen without impunity. If participants understand WHY a contributor is saying something, they won't respond emotionally. It's the facilitator's job to make sure the goal of all conversations is to determine the best possible outcomes.

Secondly, they need to undertake a simulated exercise in the process.

There are seven different learning styles: spatial, auditory, verbal, physical, logical, social and solitary. The more of these you can include, the more likely people are to retain the information.

A problem statement, defined as a description of something that is worth solving for, will immerse participants in the process. Below are some examples to get you started.

- "Do our customers wish to speak to us when complaining about one of our products"
- "How will customers purchase property in the future"
- "How can our contact centre decrease their customer effort score while maintaining satisfaction"
- "How can we better embed Risk & Regulation in our business without it being a blocker"
- "How can we better protect our personal data"
- "How can we support parents in going back to work"

You get the gist.

The next stage is to select the quantification measure that this innovation must achieve.

Allow me to drive this point home. Every organisation is governed by three key performance indicators (KPIs): its ability to increase revenue, reduce cost or reduce risks. This is true for governments and NGOs, as much as for private and public corporations. All cascading KPIs within your business will involve one or more of these three, therefore it could be argued that all innovations are driven by a step change in one of these three. If you can't do this; then why would you be pushing innovation, unless it's a PR exercise or something you feel you SHOULD be investing in?

Let's take the six problem statements we cited earlier and specify some appropriate metrics.

Problem statement	Appropriate metric
"Do our customers wish to speak to us when complaining about one of our products"	Reduce cost of complaint resolution by 15% (Cost)
"How will customers purchase property in the future"	Increase share of wallet by 10% (Revenue)
"How can our contact centre decrease their customer effort score while maintaining satisfaction"	Increase in NPS by 10% (Risk, Revenue)
"How can we better embed Risk & Regulation in our business without it being a blocker"	Reduction in project slippage of 20% (Risk)
"How can we better protect our personal data"	Increase in NPS by 10% (Risk)
"How can we support parents in going back to work"	Increase in revenue in this segment by 15% (Revenue)

The next step is to identify the assumptions that need to hold true in order to achieve this objective. Let us take the example of "How can we better support parents in going back to work". The following assumptions could underpin this.

1. That we can attract parents to our brand.
2. That our contact centre is skilled in dealing with this community.
3. That parents want to return to the workforce.
4. That parents need support.
5. That there are no significant legal impediments to working with parents.
6. That we have the buy-in of the customer success team.
7. That the board understand parents as a new strategic segment.
8. That the way we communicate with parents resonates.
9. That we have an operating model that's designed to support parents.

... and so on.

The facilitator then selects a representative of the organisation to take on the role of the parent in the mobilisation phase.

It's important that we create a sense of urgency and reduce the natural tendency for placing obstacles in front of us. In order to do so, we need to run faster than our ability to allow negative thoughts to intervene. We do this by having a half-day mobilisation in which the innovation team and the parent role immerse themselves in the process. Hour 1 for Mobilisation, Hour 2 for Understanding the Need, Hour 3 for Meet the Need and Hour 4 for Facilitate the Need.

The next step is to identify the right vertical segments. Let me describe what that means.

If your organisation is at scale and profitable, you are already excellent at horizontal segmentation. That is defining a group of existing customers based on demographic. Examples include high-net-worth individuals, millennials, baby boomers and old-age pensioners. If you already have some form of Design Thinking in place, then you are familiar with personas. For example, a persona for a music company will look something like this:

"As a *student, living at home in London,*
I want to *have choice in the music I listen to."*

Personas are useful for 'I want to future-proof' and 'I want to fix' type innovations as the unmet need is quite explicit. In other words, it has already been defined either in the marketplace or within your own organisation. In the case of 'I want to find the next big thing' you are in the world of implicit unmet needs, meaning your potential customers may not know what they do not know, so you have to extract it from them. Here's an example from my own life:

As a 38-year-old gentleman, I've given up on close shaving. I made the transition to electric razors about four years ago and have never looked back. This buying decision appears to be straightforward - get rid of an old Gillette razor and buy a new electric razor.

In actuality, it's much more complex. Our brain processes words at 2,500 a minute and imagery at one every 12 milliseconds, therefore our ability to process information internally is much greater than, say, talking (which is around 250 words a minute). The 'fast information' informs the implicit decision-making process. It would go something like this:

1. Realise I don't need to close shave everyday (this is called the First Thought).
2. Recognise that the right alternative is an electric shaver.
3. Remember that my previous experience with an electric shaver caused sensitivity.
4. Be self-aware enough to know I'm impatient and it needs to charge fairly quickly.
5. Realise that I travel significantly.
6. Understand that I want a five o'clock shadow, not a beard.

When we investigate this, it becomes apparent that we hire purchases and companies to do a job for us. In this case, I bought the electric razor to do the six jobs I've just mentioned.

We will revisit the implicit journey in the next chapter in terms of the outcomes we might expect and the importance of the first thought. Would a horizontal segment really information this 'electric razor' journey - I do not think so.

So, what do we do? Well, we need a horizontal segment and a vertical segment. The horizontal segment may be demographic-based, so an example would be 'males, aged 35-40'. The vertical segment would be must more specific: 'razor users and travel for work'. We need ten horizontal and ten vertical segments for this method. If you've already done horizontal segmentation to death, this pre-existing information can be used to inform the method. Let's summarise.

Aviva is a British multinational insurance company that is 20 years old, has 30,000 employees and services about 33 million customers. Insurance companies, as regulated entities have developed operating models that are highly compliant but not always flexible and are traditionally slow to bring innovation to the marketplace. Aviva showed their mobilisation prowess by bringing a product to the marketplace that gave free life insurance cover worth £15,000 to new parents from the time their child is born to the time they are in pre-school. Genius!

Stage Action List

1. Build a cross-functional innovation team.
2. Train the innovation in how to interact with customers or other employees.
3. Identify a facilitator
4. Quantify the metric you are working towards.
5. Confirm your problem statement.

Timeframe to Complete: 1-2 weeks

Stage Inputs

1. Your horizontal segmentation.
2. Executive level sponsorship.

Stage 1: Understand the Need

"Any fool can know. The point is to understand."

– Albert Einstein

The most important stage in this method is Understanding the Need. If you do not apply this thinking correctly, the result will be investing in an unmet need that is irrelevant to those you intend to attract. Before we discuss the process, let us first introduce some of the artefacts you are going to use.

Hiring Statements

If you believe that we hire organisations to do a particular job for us, then hiring statements speak to the context upon which you would hire or not hire. They're quite different to personas. Let us take the example of a bank whose problem statement is "How do we engage flexible workers in a cost-effective way". There is not really an equivalent in Design Thinking or traditional innovation approaches, but an extended persona might look like this:

Name: Tom Thumb

Age: 37

Location: San Francisco

Likes: Walks in the park, films, listening to music.

Products: Mortgage, life protection, mortgage protection.

A hiring statement for this person would be along the lines of:

"When I am pursuing career goals that do not produce a steady income, I want to access financial products that are geared to my short-term needs, and advice that allows me to plan for a worst-case scenario and not worry about a pay cheque, so that I can maintain a basic level of comfort at each increment towards that goal."

As you can see, the hiring statement is based on causality - that is, the relationship between cause and effect. As you can see, the statement is more pointed and rich in emotion. It comes from the jobs canvas: don't worry if it isn't obvious how this comes together, we will speak to it in more detail later.

Outcomes

Each job canvas has a number of outcomes, which, as defined, are unmet needs that this customer requires before they will hire your organisation. Let us take the example of an electronics company that is looking to "better engage the student population using music". A persona-based approach to capturing this could be:

"**As a** *student, living at home in London,*
I want to *have choice in the music I listen to."*

Using the concept of an outcome, it would be more like:

When *I'm on the go and wish to listen to music,* **I want to** *listen to all the songs I love* **so I can** *steal a moment to myself in what is otherwise a hectic day.*

You will find more on outcomes when we talk about the jobs canvas.

Implicit Journey

Many of you will be familiar with the customer journey map in its hundreds of permutations. This depicts the process view of how a customer interacts with your organisation, identifying points of intervention and opportunities to delight. I have always found the concept of delighting the customer strange, as I cannot recall the last time I felt delight in buying a pencil or mortgage protection. That said, the premise of customer journeys is correct. They explicitly capture 'known knowns' and 'unknown knowns' in terms of how to intervene when it comes to customers. Customer journey maps are perfect for 'I want to fix' or 'I want to future-proof' type innovations.

When looking for the 'next big thing' innovations, it is all about capturing 'unknown unknowns', as customers don't know that want before they want it. We therefore require an implicit journey map, a device that captures the first thought through to the point at which the customer makes a purchase. I describe this in detail later.

Four Forces Diagram

Even if we understand the implicit journey and the vertical segment, we still need to overcome the habits that the customer has built up over time and the anxiety or emotion they may have that is only natural when we enact a change in our lives. They are two of the four forces that push a potential customer away from your innovation or pull them towards it.

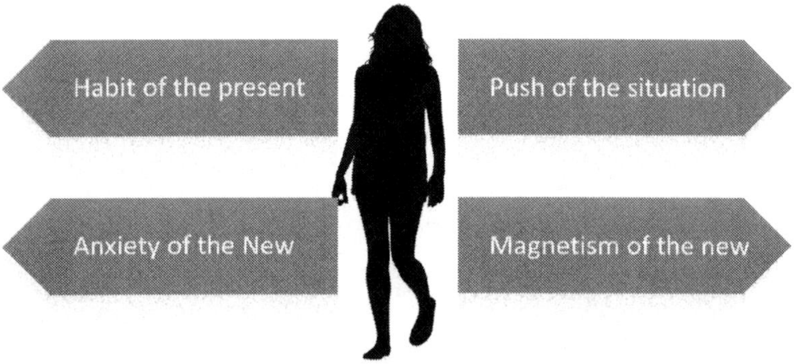

Habits of the present are things we do today that keep us wedded to our existing product and services. For example, "Our family have always banked with Citi-Bank."

Anxiety of the new are the emotions we attach to making a change. For example, "My iPhone makes me popular, I'm afraid that the Samsung won't be the same."

"Push of the situation" are thoughts that move you towards a new decision. For example, "The Xbox has a new game I really want to play."

"Magnetism of the new" is a gauge of how attractive one finds the new situation. For example, "I really want to get in shape and the Fitbit can help me do that."

Jobs Canvas

The Jobs Canvas, much like a Lean Canvas (an artefact produced in the Lean Startup method) contains all the critical elements captured during the interview. It includes four types of outcomes.

'Overserved outcomes' are products, services and innovations that the customer being interviewed is inundated with, from your organisation or one of your competitors.

'Irrelevant outcomes' are products, services or innovations that are offered to the customer, which they do not feel are necessary in deciding whether or not to hire an organisation.

'Table stake outcomes' are products, services and innovations that are not currently catered for but that the customer wishes to be catered for.

'Underserved outcomes' are products, services or innovations that are currently catered for, but the customer is dissatisfied with an aspect of them, creating an opportunity for intervention.

The Approach

The Understand the Need stage starts with the scheduling of interviews. You will interview each segment at least once, resulting in ten interviews altogether. It is vital that we do not transfer our own subjective experience into the interview process, so let's pause on that point.

I struggle to count the number of times I have heard an organisation dictate a need to a customer instead of extracting it from them. This is usually articulated quite politely by a phrase like "but… what you're really looking for here is… xxx" or "I know what customers want… they want… xxx". What might sound even crazier is that customers often respond in the positive: "Oh, yes please."

Allow me to explain this with an analogy. At the time of writing, my son Bodhi is three. He's a great kid, full of youthful energy. Most Saturdays I take him to our local grocery store, where he wants to "look and touch" the items in the toy section. As an absolute pushover, I find myself relenting. So, what do you think happens when Bodhi gets to the toy section? He wants every single toy he sees, be it Harry Potter figures, Lego or Peppa Pig sticker books. Every now and then (OK, a lot of the time), I buy him a car or something small, which keeps him busy for 20 minutes or so.

When we get home, he's excited to open the packaging of his car and spends another 20 minutes wheeling it up and down the floor, my legs, the couch or anything else that looks remotely like a road. But what happens next? The car gets put to one side and he's back playing with his train set. The same train set he played with yesterday and the 30 days before that.

My point is that if you offer customers or employees a toy shop, they're going to want everything in it. By luck or by instinct, you may get it right, but ultimately customers will go back to playing with the train set. Bodhi doesn't know why he plays with the train set, but if we could extract that information from him, we could use it to 'sell' him more train sets. This is the intention of our interview: to capture implicit buying journeys and associated required outcomes.

To do this, we need to understand the relationship between cause, effect, emotions, motivations and a particular outcome. The following pyramid will help.

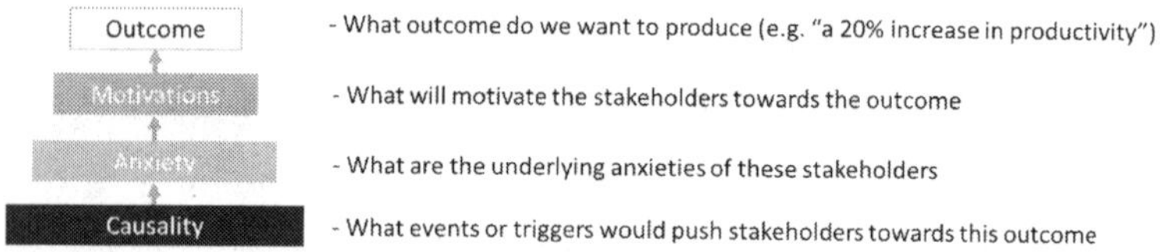

The Implicit Journey Map, which we introduced earlier; captures the causality through six distinct points in a buying journey.

The First Thought is the point at which the customer or employee has identified a need. In my razor example, the first thought would be that I no longer wanted to be clean-shaven.

Passively Looking is when someone recognises the need for change but can't yet identify what they want. This would be me looking at actors and colleagues to see what level of stubble might suit me.

Actively Looking describes the period when you're seeking to make a decision. An example would be asking my father for advice on what he uses to shave.

Deciding is the point at which you're poised to make a decision. In my case, choosing to shop at Argos because it offered convenience (it was nearby) and choice (it sold a number of electric razor brands).

Consuming was the day I bought and checked my new razor.

Experiencing is the point I'm at now. I recently purchased a new, lighter, chargeable electric razor.

The next section looks at how to extract this using interviews.

Interviews

We need to schedule interviews with each of the vertical segments. That's ten in total, each one lasting an hour, including introductions. Unlike focus groups or customer interviews, which are fit for purpose for 'I want to fix' and 'I want to future-proof' innovations, interviews for 'I want the next big thing' should not be driven with the unmet need or potential product or service at its apex.

What I mean is, it is not your job to push the new product or service on to the customer, nor to introduce bias into the response. Instead, an experienced facilitator will finesse the conversation through each of the points of the Implicit Journey. Consider the questions below.

Point	Question
First Thought	Can you remember a time when...?
Passively Looking	What did you notice around this time?
Actively Looking	Who did you bring with you when looking?
Deciding	How did you navigate the choices you have?
Consuming	Did it meet your expectations?
Experiencing	Have your preferences changed since?

Interviews need two members of the team, the facilitator plus another. It also important that sessions be limited to 60 minutes, 45 minutes of which is interview itself. The first 15 minutes are to ensure the participant is at ease and able to ask questions. The session must also be over the phone, to avoid any bias based on body language, facial responses or judgements about how you look.

An experienced facilitator's questions will move the participant from *First Thought* through to *Experienced*, as well as capturing the Four Forces. Questions might include:

Push	Can you describe a time where you changed your mind?
Pull	Would you describe yourself as routined?
Anxiety	Who do you go to for advice?
Habit	Do you normally shop in the same places?

These ten tips and tricks should help you.

1. If there is a pause, do not interrupt. You need to give the interviewee time to think. In fact, a pause can help when the interviewee appears distracted, so use it when you need to.
2. "Can you remember a time when..." starts the interview and pushes it towards the First Thought.

3. Be careful to allow space for emotional or ancillary jobs to resurface but be quick to bring the interviewee back on track when they meander.
4. Create rapport by starting sentences with disarming phrases such as "with your permission" or "may I ask".
5. Choose the simplest language.
6. Use 'specifically' to extract details. "Can you specifically tell us what you were considering in that moment?"
7. When discussing an event that led to a buying decision, always ask who was with them and how they got there.
8. Don't ask leading questions.
9. Pay attention to tone of voice.
10. Paraphrase and reflect to ensure you understand.

At the end of the interview, thank them for their time, then send a follow-up note that lays out the next steps.

Sometimes the most innocuous statement can give us insights into the implicit buying process, so it's important for the second member of the team to record the interview. This requires consent, but I have never heard anyone say no.

Next, we need to account for the *Four Forces*.

In the electric razor example, a number of forces informed my buying decision. First, I was used to removing stubble with shaving cream and a razor - it was a routine for me. Gillette has strong brand loyalty, and I did feel the brand updated its product range in my favour, so that was pulling me back. I have sensitive skin, however, and using a razor daily was taxing, so I was skipping days, pushing me towards a change. In addition, the fact I could go to Argos and choose from more than two dozen electric razors was quite compelling.

We can summarise these forces on a template, modified from the good work Bob Moesta and his team do at the ReWired Group...

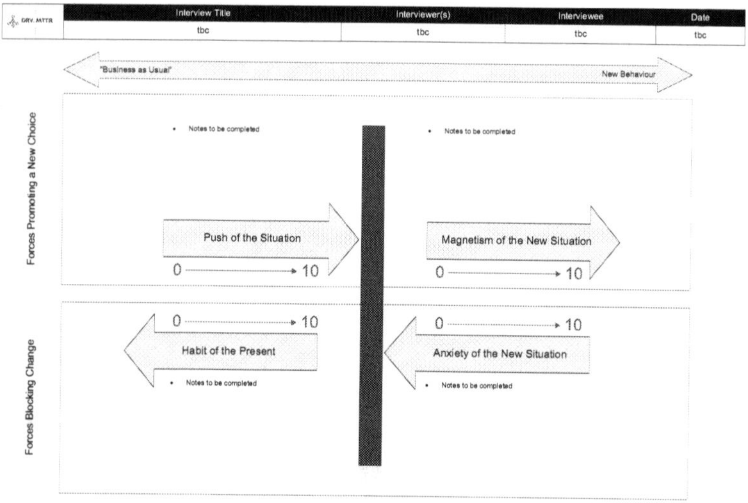

Once it's drafted, we'll give a score of one to ten to each of the *Four Forces*. If the forces blocking change produce a significantly higher figure than those leading to a new choice, this may allude to the habits of the present being stronger than the product or service you are investigating.

This aggregates upwards to an Implicit Journey map. With experience, you will be able to draft this while the interview is taking place. The following is the template we use.

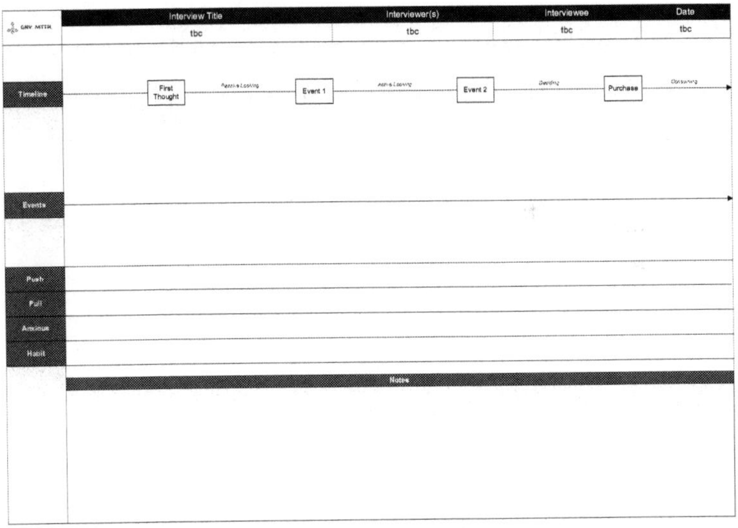

This template is a time-bound view. It takes the notes you have made in the Four Forces diagram and applies Push, Pull, Anxiety and Habit to each event that led to a buying decision. At the end of each phase - *Passively*

Looking, Actively Looking, Deciding, Committing and *Experienced* - an event or number of events will move the customer or employee to the next phase. Listen out for these, as they are points at which you can intervene. I have found the closer you do so to the *First Thought*, the lower the cost and the stronger the probability of creating brand advocacy. The Mobilisation Phase is important to hone the team's ability to listen and not just hear in completing the *Implicit Journey.*

We now have an *Implicit Journey* and a *Four Forces* diagram. The final part of the Understand the Need stage is to capture the output in a *Jobs Canvas,* derived from Tony Ulwich's *Jobs to be Done Canvas*. The *Jobs Canvas* is work in progress until the Facilitate the Need stage and not all vertical segments (and therefore Job Canvases) will make it through this stage.

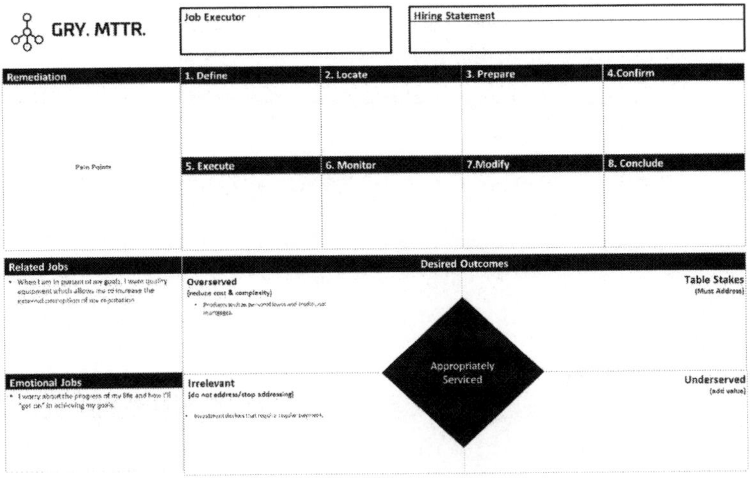

Figure 4: Derived from here: https://jobs-to-be-done.com/the-jobs-to-be-done-canvas-f3f784ad6270

The Job Executor, as you would imagine, is the vertical segment under interview. You place your Hiring Statement adjacent to the vertical segment. This statement is like a Design Principle. When a disagreement occurs, the *Hiring Statement* can be used to test any assumptions being made. This also marks the first time several additional concepts emerge.

Remediations

Remediations are emotional touch points wedded to bad experiences that come out of the interview. This may be waiting on the phone too long when making a complaint, or not receiving an auto-response when the segment completed an online application. We capture these, as each is a point of intervention for a positive experience (see 'delighting customers' earlier).

Define - Conclude

This section speaks to the operational process and is tailored to the domain of your industry and the problem statement. For example, in retail you may have something more akin to the Funnel with steps for Awareness, Prospecting, Engagement and Purchasing. Often, in addition to the *Implicit Journey*, you will find interviewees touch upon insightful aspects of their current purchasing journey. This section allows you to capture these elements, which can then be fed into the Facilitate the Need stage. Do not worry if this is empty, as the other sections should take preference.

Desired Outcomes

The most important section on the canvas is the Desired Outcomes, which fall into four categories: Overserved, Underserved, Table Stakes and Irrelevant. Outcomes are in the form of

> "When............I (Don't) Want To.........So I Can....." or
> (Situation).......(Motivation)......(Expected Outcome).

For example:

Overserved

- For a print media company: **When** I am at the train station, **I don't want** to read a newspaper, **so I can** concentrate on reading news on my phone.

Underserved

- For a coffee company: **When** I am in the need of coffee, **I want to** use my own cup, so I can save the planet.

Table Stakes

- For a bank: **When I am** in a bank branch, **I want** help with my children, **so I can** concentrate on the transaction I want to make.

Irrelevant

- For a train station: **When I** am waiting for my train, **I don't want** to get pamphlets, **so I can** have my hands free.

This should not turn into a 'round peg in a square hole' problem. If you need to amend the text to suit the outcome, do so. The main point is to describe the situation, the motivation and the outcomes in that order.

Related Job

Often in the course of an interview, other jobs will come up that produce an emotional response. In this section, you capture them. These can lead to adjacent innovations. For example, I was working with a financial services organisation and interviewing some new parents. In conversation, the interviewee complained that after work, they had only an hour with their children before the kids had to go to bed. The outcomes went something like: "**When I** get home from work, **I want to** spend quality time with my children **so I can** feel like I have imparted advice, rewarded good behaviour and been a good parent." Out of this related job came a tablet-enabled application that empowered parents to reward their children for better financial management.

Emotional Jobs

In this section, you capture anything that created an emotional response. Listen for phrases like "I hate it when", "I really appreciate" and "Do you know what I love doing?" The aim is to better understand the anxieties that are prevalent in the interviewee's life and so better understand the emotions of causality. The American chocolate giant Hershey's, for example, launched Hershey's Minis after discovering that the cups' foil wrappers created a guilt-inducing consumption. Genius!

You can expect 20 to 50 outcomes and a Hiring Statement per vertical segment, therefore ten interviews could produce as many as 500 outcomes. This is far too many to bring into the *Meet the Need* stage, so the priority is to combine similar outcomes or outcomes that are complementary. You then ask each of the five members of the innovation team to 'gut check' the outcomes, based on their prevalence to the problem you are solving. You should come together as a team and whittle the combined outcomes down to 50. When combined, these can be brought into the Meet the Need workshop.

Established in 1986, American Girl manufactures 46cm high-quality dolls, has more than 1,900 employees and achieves revenues of about $350 million a year. Researching its customer market, it identified a demographic that would buy from a company that understood the following: that owning a doll was about more than just play; that traditionally, dolls were handed down through generations; and that often, their owners created backstories and characters for them. The firm subsequently launched a doll that represents different times and places in US history, boxed with a book that tells each doll's backstory. Genius!

Chapter Summary

Stage Action List

1. Schedule interviews with at least ten verticals.
2. Complete the Four Forces Diagram and score.
3. Complete the Implicit Journey.
4. Draft the Job Canvas.

5. Combine and prioritise the Outcomes.

Timeframe to Complete: 2 Weeks

Stage Inputs

1. Your vertical segmentation.
2. A well-trained innovation team.
3. The problem statement.
4. Your quantified metric.

Step 2: Meet the Need

"Design is intelligence made visible."

– Alina Wheeler

The thought of coming face-to-face with your customers (and in many organisations, the employees) can be daunting. I worked with a US client that insisted on bringing the innovation team and attendees on a day's worth of grooming, specifying that men should be clean-shaven, the colour of their ties and how much ankle space woman attendees should show. The premise is understandable, but it scared the life out of the team, which made for a nervous Meet the Need session.

Whereas a suit is a sign of professionalism, casual clothing is the mark of a creative innovator. This session should feel like your junior school art class: authentic personality and transparency play a key role in creating a trusting environment conducive to real opinions. The running order of the Meet the Need workshop should be as follows.

9am - 9.30am: The Art of Storytelling

The innovation team sponsor from your organisation should choose a story that has been pivotal to your success (and if you're really brave, failure). It needs to be a true story and authentic to the brand.

Once, at a shareholder meeting, Stuart Gulliver - then CEO of HSBC bank in the UK - was asked why First Direct, a subsidiary, had not invested in automation technologies to reduce costs. These days, he tells of how consultants and his own team were badgering him to move away from a contact centre strategy, which meant every call "had to be answered by a person the first time". He then talks about 9/11, when a woman rang First Direct before jumping from the World Trade Center. Why? Because she knew that someone would answer the phone. While she was talking, the incredibly well-trained staff member was arranging to call her home, contacting the emergency services and attempting to counsel her in her final moments. I'm bowled over by this story every time I hear it. Stories bring organisations to life; what is your organisation's story?

In addition to the innovation team, you may want to consider inviting influencers to the Meet the Need workshop. These can include project managers from transformation programmes, chief marketing officers, your analytics team or heads of change. It's important to note that their primary role is to listen and learn. You will also invite the customers who specified the *Jobs* and/or *Outcomes* that you have deemed a priority to this stage. From experience, you should plan to invite five out of the ten vertical segments you interviewed. You will also need a second facilitator from the innovation team. In total, that means 20 to 25 participants. The running order for the day would be as follows.

9.45am - 10.45am: The Affinity Stone (Get it?)

In the affinity exercise, you separate staff and participants into two groups and ideally into two rooms (or separate sides of the same room). You will have printouts of the combined outcomes, and on the walls place five columns of MoSCoW prioritisation: **M**ust Have, **S**hould Have, **C**ould Have, **W**ould like to Have. You then ask each group to order the outcomes by priority and place them under the appropriate column. This task should take 20 minutes maximum but requires two facilitators: one to arbitrate each group. The last ten minutes is when the two groups are brought together. It's always interesting to see the internal versus external view of what is important. You then choose the top one to three outcomes across each of the two groups as input to the design session.

11am - 12.30am: Design Sprint 1

To prepare the wall for the Design session, you need to create a number of columns. The first is the outcome you are working on; the next contains the characteristics it must encapsulate; the next is a wireframe; and the last is the unique selling point, which can be defined as the one thing we need to get right so that customers or employees will use this. Let's work through an example.

The Outcome

For the sake of an example, let's choose one that might be familiar to a well-known streaming service: "**When** I'm on the go and wish to listen to music, **I want to** listen to all the songs I love **so I can** steal a moment to myself in what is otherwise a hectic day." This outcome is a combination of three outcomes: "When I'm on the go I wish to listen to music", "I want to listen to all the songs I love" and "I want to steal a moment to myself in what is otherwise a hectic day" created at the Understand the Need stage.

The Characteristics

In the Understand the Need workshop, the customer stipulated the following characteristics: "I want it to be... interactive, fun, mobile, instant, works in offline, should be non-intrusive, makes recommendations, free, does not require signal, does not drain my battery, playlists, private, mood-dependent, familiar, online support".

The Wireframe

Depending on the problem you are solving and the outcome you're moving towards, you will require wire-frames in the following formats: Desktop, Tablet, Mobile and Landscape & Mobile Portrait, and if it's a new proposition for employees, then a Lean Canvas template (see below)

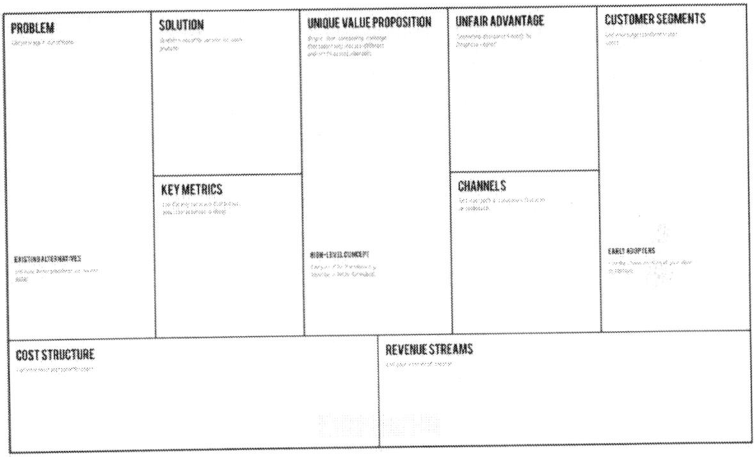

Figure 5: Reproduced from here: https://leanstack.com/leancanvas

This should take 20 minutes, which indicates the level of drawing ability you need. Over time, it would be useful to develop stencils for particular elements, such as buttons, dialogues and label boxes.

Figure 6: Reproduced from sketchize.com

The Unique Selling Point

The Unique Selling Point is the one element that needs to be true to produce traction on the product or service. In the above example, the USP was "any song I want, always available, even those I didn't know existed".

You may find that you require more than an hour, in which case restart the conversation as part of Design Sprint 2. The goal is to find the most sensible one or two outcomes in which to invest your efforts. This is no time to be polite: if you feel the outcome being worked on requires no more conversation, move on.

12.30pm - 1.30pm: Break

A break means a break. These sessions are intense and at times overwhelming. Use this time to create rapport in the group and get to know your customers or employees that bit better.

1.30pm - 3.00pm Design Sprint 2

Either Design Sprint 2 will be a continuation of Design Sprint 1 or a new sprint based on the second priority outcomes, chosen from the Affinity exercise. The exact same process remains as per Design Sprint 2.

3.00pm - 4.30pm Design Sprint 3

Either Design Sprint 3 will be a continuation of Design Sprint 2, or a new sprint based on the second priority outcomes, chosen from the Affinity exercise. The exact same process remains as per Design Sprint 1.

4.30pm - 5.00pm: Day Summary

At this point, you can excuse any external participants. Remember to thank them for their time and explain the next two stages, Facilitate the Need and Embed the Need. Add that the innovation team will consider what we've learned today, and that they may be called back for the Facilitate the Need workshop.

5.00pm - 6pm: Facilitate the Need Prioritisation

Dedicate the end of the day to prioritising the Design Sprints. We need to isolate the one or two worth considering at the Facilitate the Need Workshop. One method is the Engagement Experience Cycle, designed to put the innovation team and participants in an objective frame of mind:

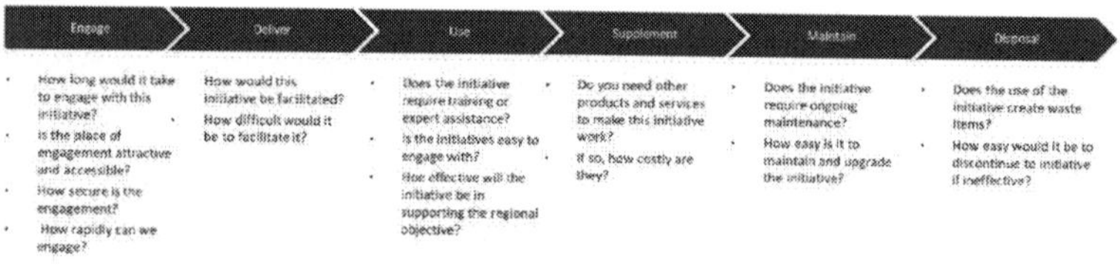

Figure 7: Engagement Experience Cycle

The second mechanism is the Feasibility, Commerciality and Desirability Venn Diagram. The evaluation questions for each of these are designed in Stage 0: Mobilisation and can vary depending on the problem statement and the domain of your organisation. Helpful questions might be:

1. Capability (the capacity of your organisation to support this intiative)
    a. Can we technically build this?
    b. It is satisfactory from a regulatory and compliance standpoint?
    c. Does it align with existing strategy and technology?
    d. When will the value be realised?
    e. Should this be Buy or Build?
2. Desirability (the level of confidence of alignment)
    a. Who wants this?
    b. Is there a desire on a global/regional/domestic level?

    c. What is the market size?
    d. Is there a willingness to pay?
3. Commerciality (the level of investment required versus the benefit)
    a. Does it represent a new revenue or sales opportunity?
    b. Does it represent a new cost savings, cost avoidance or productivity opportunity?
    c. Will it create stickiness?
    d. Does it stack up against cost:benefit?

It is useful to distribute scorecards for Capability, Desirability and Commerciality a week in advance of the session, at the same time as meeting senior representatives to discuss the questions in the Mobilisation phase. By doing so, you can reduce the time to score. Also bear in mind that the level of detail needs to satisfy all four workplace personality types.

1. The Analytical

   These types will question the questions, mull over usage of verbs, nuances in understanding and proclaim there is not enough detail to answer appropriately. To combat this, write questions without ambiguity and define any subjective terms in a glossary.

2. The Driver

   Rather than answer the questions, the Driver will quickly give an overall score and spend the rest of the time looking around, wondering why everyone else is taking so long. To combat this, create digital versions of the answer sheet that require an answer to every question before automatically calculating the score.

3. The Amiable

   These types will look to how others are responding and mimic the body language and conversations that reflect their interpretation of the questions. To combat this, participants must respond in isolation and ideally without talking (like in school).

4. The Expressive

   The Expressive will lose focus, look for patterns in the questioning (there are none!) and give answers based on their gut rather than logic. To combat this, have some feeling questions in place. For example, "The capacity of this outcome is to do me out of a job?" is always an emotive question to ask, and relevant as it affects your organisation's immune system.

Should you have more than two outcomes after this exercise, or you are a not-for-profit, or the innovation requires an assessment of the socioeconomic environment, then use Deeplist as another layer of prioritisation.

D	Demographic	✓ Where people live ✓ Who they are - age, sex, race etc. ✓ Social circumstances - education, income and lifestyle
E	Economic	✓ The extent to which the market in which you operate is prosperous (or not) and the competitive environment ✓ Factors such as taxation, monetary and competition policies of your target markets
P	Environment & Ecosystem	✓ Factors such as taxation, monetary and competition policies
L	Legal	✓ In the political landscape in which you operate (both source materials and deliver product) - what will help/ hinder operations and products?

I	Informational	✓ What data do you have? ✓ How do you use it? ✓ How is it protected? ✓ As the connected world changes with ever-increasing use of the internet and social media, what is being said about you, your market and your competitors? ✓ It is about access to information and what you can and cannot control.
S	Social	✓ The needs and wants of both target markets, social attitudes to the types of products and services you offer. ✓ How your organisation is seen by the outside world ✓ CSR - Corporate Social Responsibility
T	Technological	✓ What is changing in the world of technology that will impact your products or services? ✓ New innovations, adaptations and adoption rates of new technologies. What is changing and how fast?

Under Armour, a sport apparel company that employs more than 15,000 people and generates about $5.2 billion in yearly sales, focused on intercepting an unmet need of professional athletes. Founder Reed Hastings searched for textiles that would both increase perfor-

mance and manage sweat. Under Armour launched a whole new range of undergarments that did exactly this. HeatGear, for example, keeps athletes dry, cool and light. Genius!

Stage Action List

1. Use an Affinity Stone to draw attention to outcomes priorities.
2. Capture the characteristics of prioritised outcomes.
3. Wireframe the outcomes.
4. Set the Unique Selling Point of the outcome.
5. Prioritise for the next phase.

Timeframe to Complete: 1 week

Stage Inputs

1. Interviews of 10 Verticals
2. Four Forces Diagram and score.
3. Completed Implicit Journey.
4. Drafted Job Canvas.

Stage 3: Facilitate the Need

"The swamp is a business model,
a successful business model."

– Steve Bannon

I've said previously that organisations are like immune systems, composed of white blood cells waiting to attack foreign bodies. By the same token, innovation is a red blood cell waiting to be killed. Traditional approaches to innovation ignore the back-office functions and operating model, but processes and capabilities are key to an innovation's success.

You should now have one or two outcomes that have completed due diligence, been wireframed and have Unique Selling Points. Let's take stock of where we are in the process;

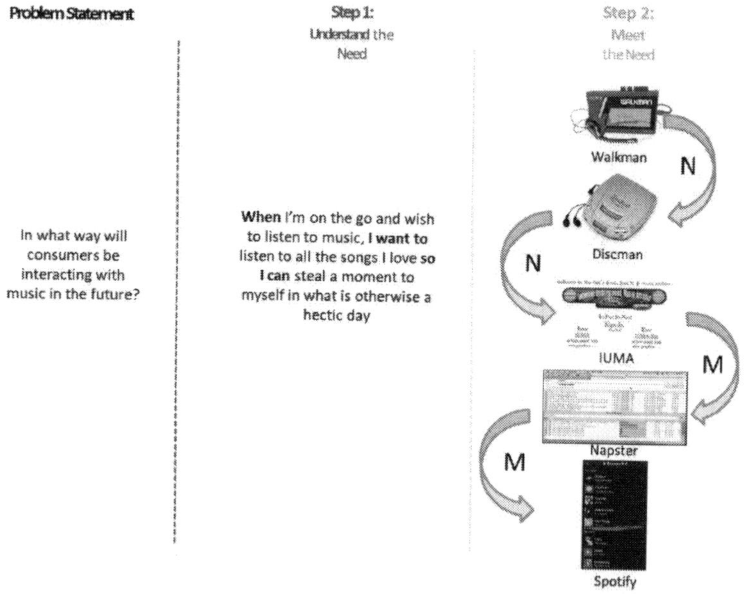

20

It's key that customer representatives for the outcome are present in the Facilitate the Need workshop. This is when we bring them face-to-face with the back-office functions they will need to support. In our example, we had the following outcome:

"When *I'm on the go and wish to listen to music,* **I want to** *listen to all the songs I love* **so I can** *steal a moment to myself in what is otherwise a hectic day."*

We defined this as requiring the following characteristics:

"Interactive, fun, mobile, instant, works in offline, should be non-intrusive, makes recommendations, free, does not require signal, does not drain my battery, playlists, private, mood-dependent, familiar, online support."

Two weeks prior to the Facilitate the Need session, you are reviewing the Jobs Canvas to determine the office functions that would be required to operate it. You may also find it useful to assign a number of the characteristics to each one. For instance:

1. Marketing (interactive, fun)
2. Digital/IT (mobile, instant)
3. IT/Infrastructure (works in offline)
4. Customer/Contact Centre (non-intrusive, mood-dependent)
5. Risk & Compliance
6. Legal
7. Content (recommendations, playlists)

In this period, it is also useful to think about your organisation's Strengths and Weaknesses, along with Market Opportunities and Threats. You may use SWOT but we have found NOISE analysis to be just as effective if not more so. The composition of NOISE is as follows:

Needs	Opportunities	Improvements	Strengths	Exceptions
If we just had ________, this would be a better place to work or we would be effective in completing our plan or *make it fit with the outcome.*	Other regions / locations / companies / teams / etc are doing ____________ An area of untapped talent OR under-utilised resources is____________. What do we currently have that could be used differently?	While you are sleeping tonight, a miracle occurs. What you need in order to be more effective at work happens, but you don't know that until you go to work tomorrow. What would you have to notice to make you realise? How would you know?	What is working well? How do you know? What is your team good at? Please give examples.	Of the needs, opportunities and improvements listed, what is already happening, even if just a little bit**?**

NOISE will help the team bring objections and improvements to the table during the Facilitate the Need workshop, thereby creating a space for shared experience.

For the workshop, you will need six hours of your day and a boardroom with a whiteboard or wall space. Sit each of the back-office representatives in the logical order of your business. For the seven we've mentioned, that would be Customer/Contact Centre -> Content -> Digital/IT -> IT Infrastructure -> Legal -> Risk & Compliance.

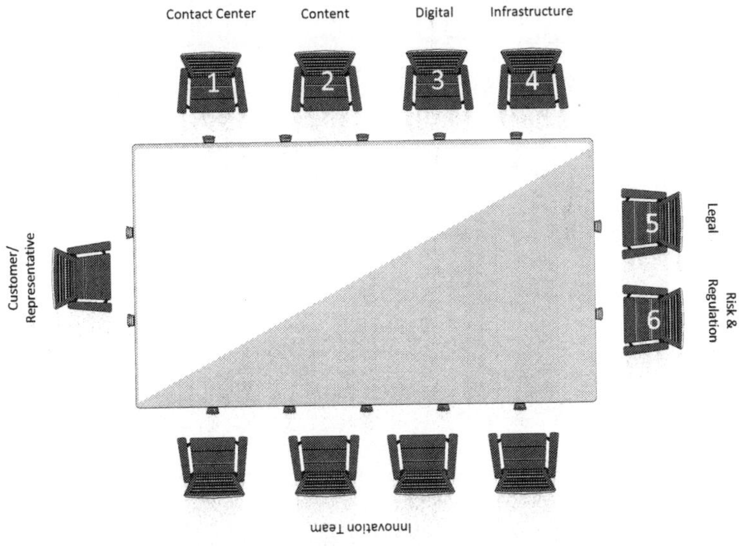

You have now found a much more pragmatic use for your boardroom, even though this structure does not feel comfortable the first time you set it up. You'll get pushback as personalities and opinions clash, but this is perfectly normal. It's the perfect representation of the organisation's mood. If staff are resigned or disgruntled, you will feel this. There is no greater example of 'storming'.

This reminds me of a session with a global retailer that was transitioning from physical shops to a more digital offer. We had a roomful of 20 people, including purchasing, payments, IT, retail executives and inventory management staff. At one point, I looked over to find one of the inventory management clerks rubbing her forehead vigorously. I might add that at the time, we were quite nosily debating the role of just-in-time inventory management.

I stopped the conversation and asked this woman for input, at which point she launched into a half-hour tirade. She spoke about how, 15 years ago, lean experts from Motorola (remember them?) took away her desk, forced her to stand and moved her further away from her house. She finished with a phrase that made me laugh heartily: the process forced her to work with "that numpty Joe who didn't have a clue!"

If you're hearing stories like this, then believe me, you're on the right track. Your attendees feel that they are in a trusted environment and have nothing to fear.

We are trying to achieve a number of objectives simultaneously here.

1. We want as many of objections, opinions or viewpoints represented in the room as possible.
2. We want to expedite the operational design in a way that ensures we do not leave space for sabotage.
3. The facilitator needs to both capture and use the customer journey to drive the conversation.
4. We want to agree an operating model that can facilitate the outcome.

Using our example, the running order for the sessions goes something like this:

Step	Description	Objective	Example	Time
1	The facilitator begins by bringing everyone to the same point, by summarising the Understand the Need and Meet the Need stages prior to socialising the outcome, characteristics, design and Unique Selling Point. He/she then asks the customer or employee representative for comment and to set the scene. The attendees introduce themselves and offer their initial impressions of the role they might take in trying to facilitate the outcome.	Ensure a shared understanding of what we are here to do.	Not applicable	30 mins
2	Ask each attendee for one reason this is not going to work. This creates a clean slate from which to start, gets participants used to communicating openly in front of potential customers and, occasionally, highlights a real obstacle to success. The facilitator places these on the parking lot.	We want to bring objections out now, not nine months into developing the solution.	"Our content is not connected to our applications".	15 mins

3	To begin with, the facilitator asks the customer: "What's the first thing you would do in interacting with this product or service?" The facilitator then asks the participants which of them deals with this task. (It's best to avoid using the words 'responsible' or 'accountable', we're trying to find the path of least resistance and they are emotive terms.) Once answered, we reshuffle the room so that this person sits in position 1. Every subsequent participant moves down one seat. At this point, you can ask for parking lot items using the earlier question, "What is the one reason this is not going to work?"	Maintain energy and through physical movement create a more complicit atmosphere.		15 mins

Repeat Step 3	In essence, we repeat Step 3 for each subsequent task in the process. The next question would be: "OK, what would you do after that?" The facilitator continually comes back to the design and the Unique Selling Point to baseline everyone's understanding, including the customer or employee representative. These artefacts were created with a much larger sample set, so are more likely to get at the truth.	Complete the journey map.		2-4 hours.
Step 4	By now, nobody is sitting in the seat they started in, and you have a level 0 To-Be operating model. The facilitator's role is to walk back through the processes captured on the wall, seeking the participants' validation.	Ensure the level 0 operating model is accurate.		30 mins
Step 5	The final step is to validate the parking lot with two questions. "Are there any obstacles that we have not accounted for?" "Have we provided solutions, or do solutions exist for any of these obstacles?"	To capture as many potential objections as possible.		30 mins

As you can see, the Facilitate the Need workshop takes six hours in total - a day in all, including breaks. What we have now is an operating model that can plausibly support the new or augmented product and service. Most importantly, we have a list of all the obstacles to meeting the metrics we defined as part of Mobilisation.

Let's discuss why these obstacles are important. In most 'transformation' programmes, particularly those that start with technology, objections arise far too late and lead to write-offs. Initially, the programme manager creates a statement of work featuring all the known risks that can occur, most of which are ignored until they become issues.

Issues arise at a number of points in a timeline, such as when new stakeholders are added to the mix, when other projects are exposed, as a piece of technology approaches going live, as people change roles, or as shareholders and board expectations change. The cost of these issues is astronomical but because they arise in iterations, we often underestimate them.

It is estimated that the cost of failure in this model will be as high as $3 trillion by 2020. We capture obstacles at source in order to deal with 80% of these scenarios, which may arise at a later stage of the change programme. In doing so, we bring them to the forefront, at a stage where it's cost-effective to deal with them in an environment where this can be done safely. This is part of the Embed the Need phase's purpose, to deal with these obstacles.

To keep the discussion reasonable, the facilitator should follow these tips:

1. There are no difficult people, just people who are different.
2. There are no irrational people, just people who see the world differently.
3. People are always trying their best to address or cope with a particular situation.
4. How flexible you are will dictate how flexible they are.
5. We cannot influence unless we listen and understand first.
6. People will change their position, and you can influence them in doing so.

The next part of the Facilitate the Need stage is to revisit the metric we defined as part of the Mobilisation phase. Let's continue with the outcome we have been using.

"**When** *I'm on the go and wish to listen to music,* **I want to** *listen to all the songs I love* **so I can** *steal a moment to myself in what is otherwise a hectic day."*

Our current revenues are $10 million, and we set ourselves the lofty target of growing revenue by 20%. That is value in the region of $2 million that needs to be created by the product we have created to meet this outcome. We identified Marketing, Digital/IE, Infrastructure, Customer/Contact Centre, Risk & Compliance, Legal and Content as key stakeholders in this process, and we now have an operating model that will work to support his. Let's consider what assumptions might be against each department and reference the current KPIs to show the delta.

Department	Revenue assumption	Current baseline	Delta
Marketing	Leads generated increase by 20%	10%	+20%
Digital	Conversation rate needs to be 8%	0%	+ 8%
Infrastructure	Four release cycles required per year	2	+ 2
Customer/ Contact Centre	10 calls answered an hour	20	-10
Risk & Compliance	Number of complaints at 5%	14%	+ 9%
Legal	15 new content licences secured	3	+ 12
Content	Catalogue increased by 20%	5%	+ 15%

To increase profit by $2 million, we need another 20% in leads and 15% in catalogue. We will also require a totally new way of converting online customers to meet the 8% target. We represent this in a repurposed House of Quality called The GRID. Before looking at it, it's worth considering a number of principles.

KPIs should not be taken in isolation

It is often assumed that KPIs set at departmental level can work in a silo, and sometimes this is the case. But given that we have just spent six hours proving the opposite, by creating an environment for crossworking, we also need to understand that KPIs in relation to innovation are interlinked and affect each other.

Take our goal of reducing the number of complaints in relation to the new service from 14% to 5%. The Contact Centre currently handles complaints and we have a target of ten calls answered an hour on this team. In order to meet both, we have to see how these two KPIs are interrelated.

Not all KPIs have a positive effect on each other.

If you're like most people, you work in an organisation that is attempting to increase revenue, reduce cost and reduce risk simultaneously. I'm not saying that's not possible with the right level of governance, but the idea that all KPIs have a positive effect on each other is incorrect. It is possible that in pursuing one KPI, we can negatively affect another.

Take the example of increasing our Marketing lead generation by 20%. The campaigns we create may be based on a service promise that has the potential to increase complaints, based on the premise that the more customers we have, the more complaints we might attract. Hence our investment in Marketing leads may increase complaints.

Now's the time to take a punt at your competitors' KPIs

Yes, I know that I said concentrating on your competitors would force you to fall over the gate. This is true in new product and service delivery - however, if possible, it's useful to benchmark your KPIs in relation to your competitors. You do not need to know the actual numbers, but being able to rank your top five competitors in order is helpful in understanding where you sit.

We represent each of these principles in The GRID. This helps us to illustrate the KPIs, how they relate to each other, the correlation (i.e. if it's a positive or negative effect) and how you position in line with competitors. The GRID consists of four sections: let's walk through each.

Section 1: The legend and the correlation.

The legend for the GRID is shown below with the first section of the correlation.

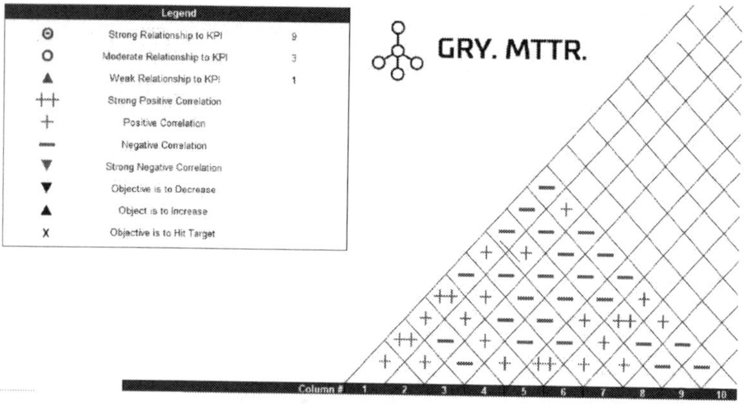

The numbered columns refer to each of the ten KPIs. Each '++', '+' and '-' stipulates the correlation between the KPIs based on 'Strong Positive', 'Positive', 'Positive', 'Negative' or 'Strong Negative'. You follow the symbols diagonally up, then diagonally back down to determine the correlation. You will note that KPI 1 has a positive correlation to KPI 2 but a negative correlation to KPI 6, we can follow the same logic across the other eight KPIs.

Section 2: The outcomes and KPIs.

The next section in the GRID is where we describe the outcomes under evaluation and the KPIs we need to manage. We also denote the level of importance of the outcomes and the correlation to each of the operational KPIs.

Row #	Max Relationship Value in Row	Relative Weight	Weight / Importance	Desired Outcomes / Associated Business KPI's	KPI 1	KPI 2	KPI 3	KPI 4	KPI 5	KPI 6	KPI 7	KPI 8	KPI 9	KPI 10
1	9	7.6	9.0	Outcome 1	⊙	▲	O	O	▲	O	O	▲	▲	▲
2	9	2.5	3.0	Outcome 2	▲	▲	⊙	⊙	▲	O	▲	▲	▲	▲

Let us run though each column. 'Max Relationship Value in Row' sets the upper limit of the scoring mechanism for 'Weight/Importance'. A value of nine indicates that the maximum weighting we can apply is nine, meaning very important. The weighting should be based on the evaluation completed in the Meet the Need stage. We calculate Relative Weighting on the basis of the 'Weight/Importance' denoted against each outcome. Each of the symbols represent the relationship between the Outcome and each of the KPIs. For example, Outcomes 1 and KPI 2 have a weak relationship, while Outcome 1 and KPI 1 have a strong relationship. A weak relationship means that an improvement to that KPI will have little effect on the outcome, and vice versa for strong relationships.

Section 3: The target KPI and Difficulty

The bottom section of the GRID depicts the target we are looking to achieve against each of the operational KPIs and the relative level of difficulty achieving it.

Target or Limit Value	KPI 1 Target	KPI 2 Target	KPI 3 Target	KPI 4 Target	KPI 5 Target	KPI 6 Target	KPI 7 Target	KPI 8 Target	KPI 9 Target	KPI 10 Target
Difficulty (0=Easy to Accomplish, 10=Extremely Difficult)	5	3	2	5	8	6	2	3	8	5
Max Relationship Value in Column	9	1	9	9	1	3	3	1	1	1
Weight / Importance	71.2	10.2	45.8	45.8	10.2	30.5	25.4	10.2	10.2	10.2
Relative Weight	26.4	3.8	17.0	17.0	3.8	11.3	9.4	3.8	3.8	3.8

It is in this section that you describe the Target or Limit to be applied against each KPI. Under that, we define the level of difficulty in achieving this on scale from 0 (Easy to Accomplish) to 10 (Extremely Difficult to Accomplish). We have a column view of the maximum value of the relationship between the KPI and the correlated outcomes. Finally, it shows the combined Weight/Importance of that KPI and the Relative Weighting in relation to the other KPIs listed.

Section 4: The Competitive Landscape

The final section is where we describe the competitor landscape in relation to each of the outcomes.

Competitive Analysis
(0=Worst, 5=Best)

Competitor 1	Competitor 2	Completitor 3	Competitor 4	Competiror 5	
1	2	3	4		
2	3	4	5		

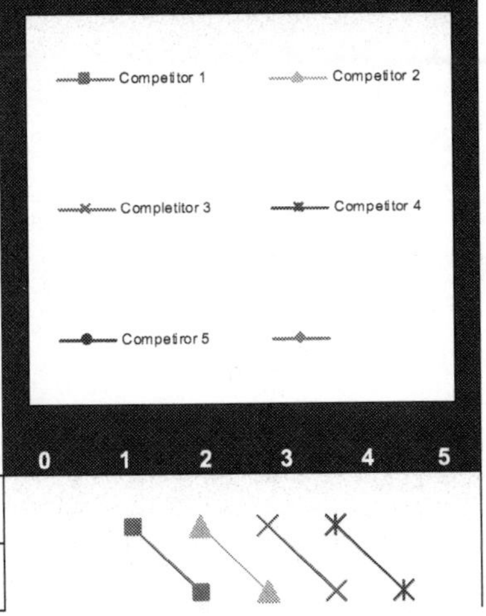

Each competitor is numbered by their position in relation to other competitors using the values 1 through 5. This is completed for each outcome, then illustrated across all outcomes in the bottom right.

The GRID is a KPI execution and monitoring plan on a page and should form part of the package presented at the end of the Embed the Need phase.

Messaging services software provider Intercom is 18 years old and valued at over $1 billion. Its 'magic' is its ability to facilitate a number of functionalities on one platform. Since its launch, its integrated messaging platform has acquired more than 100,000 active users. Key experience features include tracking of users, grouping, *auto messaging, mobile notifications and message personalisation - all facilitated through this single platform. Genius!*

Stage Action List

1. Capture all obstacles to success and validate against the driving metrics.
2. Capture the As-Is Operating Model
3. Define the To-Be Operating Model
4. Complete the GRID

Time to Complete: 2 weeks.

Stage Inputs

1. The prioritised outcomes
2. The characteristics
3. The Unique Selling Point
4. The output from the Affinity Stone exercise.

Stage 4: Embed the Need

"The single biggest problem in communication is the illusion that it has taken place."

- GEORGE BERNARD SHAW

You know the scenario. You hire the expensive consultants, they produce a beautiful report that appears plausible and robust when it's presented, the workshops finish and the consultants leave. Then objections are raised, momentum dissipates and you find the report years later in a drawer. It is in the Embed the Need phase that our commitment to developing this new or augmented product/service is tested.

The first step is to take the objections that made it through the Facilitate the Need stage and solutionise them. The four types of solutioning are Circumvention, Eradication, Consolation and Acceptance, illustrated here:

Objection	Raised By	Solution Type	Solution
From a GDPR stand-point, we cannot capture an email address without consent.	Legal	Circumvention	Confirm that email addresses are not required to facilitate playlists.
There is no integration between the content systems for songs and our customer database.	Infrastruc-ture	Consolation	For version 1, we can use RPA as a stopgap while we work on an API solution.
Our contact centre team is not trained in web support.	Contract Centre	Eradication	The digital team has agreed to train the contact centre in how to operate webchat support. The contact centre lead will assign a project manager to build out training and standard operating proce-dures.

Our digital team has no slots available to develop this technology.	Digital	Consolation	The Head of Digital will review current resource requirements and a hiring plan for contractors to support delivery. Separately, they will work with the Innovation Team around a hybrid model of delivery that will allow for customer testing outside of the standard cycle.
Our content policy does not allow a song's distributor details to be made public.	Compliance	Acceptance	In compliance with current policy, we will not share distributor details on the app.

Now that we have a good idea of how we can work through obstacles, we start creating a deployment pack. This consists of:

1. An Agile EPIC & Working Practices

   The Agile EPIC describes the body of work that the accumulated tasks will refer to. In our case, we use outcome as the title for the EPIC "**When** I'm on the go and wish to listen to music, **I want to** listen to all the songs I love **so I can** steal a moment to myself in what is otherwise a hectic day". Each EPIC is made up of a number of user stories. The format for user stories is:

   "As a < type of user >, I want < some goal > so that < some reason >"

   This can seem like a daunting task, so try to categorise your user stories by the characteristics stipulated in the Understand the Need stage and driven out in the Facilitate the Need stage. An example of a user story for fun might be:

   "As a music listener, I want to hear songs in random order, so that I never get bored".

   You will have a number of user stories against your EPIC. The objective is to close the distance between the innovation work that has brought you to this point and the effort required to see the new or augmented product or service through to completion.

These EPICs form part of a product planning process that estimates the effort to complete each story and ultimately the EPIC.

The second component is Agile working practices. The new operating model designed during Facilitate the Need required new ways of working to ensure continuous improvement and cross-collaboration. The most cost-effective way to do this is to introduce a matrix structure. Each participant will maintain their direct-line reporting, but will also have a second dotted line into a team made of up of their colleagues involved in operating the innovation. This team will be governed with different processes and capabilities than the direct line organisation governed by the following principles.

a. In the first month of operation, a SCRUM meeting will take place at close of play every day to discuss three items. It's 15 minutes long, with each team member stating how they feel the process is going and what could be improved. At the end of the month, the team decides whether it should continue with the SCRUM meetings.

b. The team has joint responsibility for continuously improving the process, with decision-making autonomy. The innovation team will offer support via a continuous improvement meeting once a month.

c. This team has no leaders. Accountability for achieving an uplift in profit or revenue, or a reduction in cost, is shared between members.

d. The innovation team is the escalation point and is there to support this new team's development.

2. An Explainer Video

In this stage of the methodology, you are fully immersed in the process and have intimate knowledge of the product or service you are producing. This is a benefit and a curse: you have the confidence (or overconfidence, watch out for that!) to know how to see it through, but explaining it to someone who has not been part of the process may be difficult. One-minute explainer videos are your friend here, since the cost of producing one is significantly less than the confusion that can arise when you don't. You can script an explainer video as follows:

1. Start by providing a 200-word description of the product or service.
2. Describe your target audience based on the vertical segment.
3. Describe why you are creating the video and the level of profit or revenue you wish to see, or the level of cost or risk you are aiming to reduce.

4. Describe the hiring statement.
5. Describe the characteristics.
6. What is the Unique Selling Point that we are looking to achieve?
7. Design a slogan for your product or service (this is the fun part).

You may have an internal marketing team who can produce this, but there are plenty of cost-effective external options too.

3. The Customer Journey Workbook

The Customer Journey Workbook is the bible of the entire process. It contains a number of items, including the level 0 customer journey map created in Facilitate the Need, all your Job Canvases, the vertical segments, any objections raised (with responses) and the quantification and associated assumptions made in the Mobilisation Stage.

This workbook travels with the Agile EPIC. The participants and the innovation team will sign it off, because it's more than likely that any objections raised as we operationalise this innovation have already been discussed. In having a record of this discussion and the artefacts that surround it, you can move much quicker through the obstacle and back to working.

Credit Suisse, a Swiss international investment bank and financial services company, is more than a century old and employs 45,000 people. It developed Digipigi, an amazing product geared towards the hard-to-reach parent-and-child market. Kids can set and track saving goals, while parents can pay out pocket money and agree on a reward for chores or behaviours. Digipigi responds with facial and sound expressions. In terms of embedding, the project involved a large number of diverse stakeholders from across the group: everyone from Marketing to Legal to IT to Product. The effort to do so at scale should not be underestimated. Genius!

Figure 8: Reproduced from http://alumni.mba.unisg.ch/entrepreneurial-alumni-makes-financial-literacy-fun/

Stage Action List

1. Complete the Explainer Video
2. Consolidate all project artefacts
3. Draft Agile EPIC
4. Transition to the Build Team.

Time to Complete: 2 weeks.

Stage Inputs

1. The GRID
2. The TO-BE Operating Model
3. The Jobs Canvas
4. The Implicit Journey
5. Prioritised Outcomes

What Now?

"Motivation is the art of getting people to do what you want them to do because they want to do it."

– Dwight D. Eisenhower

If you have made it this far, I thank you for sticking it out. Each of you will now respond in accordance with your interpretation of reality. Remember that your nervous system will be preparing your body for either rest or action, so choose action.

I have heard it all. "We're not a start-up," "This is too complex," "Our organisation isn't mature enough for something like this," "We've tried this before." I have also watched dozens of organisations like yours start fearfully and produce outstanding results. As you work through this method, you can expect to see your organisation's narrative change. It may look something like this:

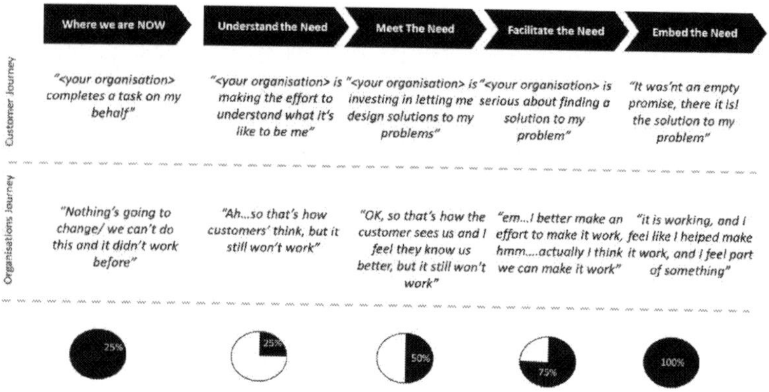

We can ask ourselves a number of questions as we move on to the next steps. I've created a readiness assessment for organisations such as yours here: www.grymttr.org/readiness.

A positive result of this is readiness for mobilisation. The first step here is either identifying individuals in your organisation who are predisposed to innovation, or looking for external help. Should you choose the latter option, one challenge is to select the right partner.

Ideally in a partner-based approach, you will identify an innovation leader who can work full time with your partner and will progress into taking a lead role in future iterations. The maturity argument is an excuse, not a reason, the right partner will be flexible to your cultural nuances.

Look, I know the fear. Not wanting to rock the boat, being conscious of your standing within your organisation, feeling resigned ("We tried this before") and not wanting to be the only one swimming against the tide. But, as I suggest later in this book, no change comes from comfort. Think of the human rights movement, the suffragettes, the passing of healthcare legislation, Brexit or the European smoking ban.

Think of any new habit you have formed: giving up smoking, giving up drinking, losing weight or doing all three. Think of any time you've received feedback and reacted defensively. All of these are life-changing experiences, but all stem from a period of discomfort.

None of the companies mentioned in this book are nimble start-ups. They have the same political, cultural and organisational challenges as you and me. If they can be successful in innovation, so can you. The most powerful person in any room is the one who will have no truck with defeat. Make a deal with yourself that this is part of your journey towards being that person.

The most impressive statistic I have seen came from a global financial services organisation that was on track to cut costs by 60%, using innovation to drive sustainability and simplification. And if we move beyond innovation's effect on the bottom line, it's important to remember that each of these companies has created a culture of innovation that is now at its very core.

Success is a new product, service or proposition that generates returns in the 3:1 to 5:1 range and GRID KPIs that you are monitoring through to completion. I wish you luck on your journey.

Who am I and why should you trust me?

I have had my fair share of success and failure. For nearly two decades, I have also worked with organisations that strive to achieve something. Back in 2006, when I was a youngster, I was advised that to test the boundaries of your comfort zone, you should always feel like "you're about to get fired". Being fired is probably a step too far. Nevertheless, this is a common attitude among those who've taught me the most. They are always pushing boundaries.

Two of the greatest skills one can learn are to be curious and to listen. By doing both, I've come to value integrity, quality, thinking and continuous improvement, which I'm pleased to say has seen me recognised by CEO Today, WWL and Acquisition International magazine as a thought leader in the areas of digital and innovation. It has also led me on the path to this book, and the Accelerating Innovation. I believe innovation and innovation centres of excellence should be profit not cost centres, and if you are not holding them accountable for affecting the bottom line of your business, then it's nothing more than a public relations exercise.

As Harvard professor Clay Christensen - the father of disruptive innovation - often says, you don't have to trust me, but trust the theory and whether it applies to your unique circumstances. Earlier in this book, I talk about the importance of objectivity, but a leader's capacity to assess and be resilient in the face of objections is directly proportional to their ability to drive real change. This is particularly prevalent in an age where the only thing moving faster than technology innovation is customer expectation.

About GRY. MTTR.

GRY.MTTR is reinventing consulting and specialises in Innovation, Automation and Risk, Regulation and Security, empowering our workforce through a proprietary platform that assures the right team at the right time at the right price. You can contact us anytime info@grymttr.org

Further reading

Cable, D. (2018). *Alive at Work.* Boston, Massachusetts: Harvard Business Review Press.

Carayol, R. (2017). SPIKE, strengths, positively, identified, kick-start, excellence. London, United Kingdom. LID Publishing.

Spiek, Chris, et al. *"Mastering Jobs-To-Be-Done Interviews."* Mastering Jobs to Be Done Interviews, #JTBD, 12 September 2019, learn.jobstobedone.org/courses/JTBDinterviews.

Ulwick, Tony. *"Jobs to be Done + Outcome Innovation"*, Medium, 12 September 2019, jobs-to-be-done.com/@Ulwick

Ulwich, A. (2015): *"What Customer's Want: Using Outcome Driven Innovation to Create Breakthrough Products and Services"*, London, United Kingdom, McGraw-Hill Education.

Kay, F. and Kite, N. (2009). *Understanding NLP*. London, United Kingdom. Kogan Page Ltd

Knapp, J., Zeratsky, J. and Kowitz, B. (2016). *Sprint*. London, United Kingdom, Transworld Publishers Ltd.

Ries, E. (2019). *The Lean Startup: How Constant Innovation Creates Radically Successful Businesses*. London: Penguin Books Ltd.

Christensen, C. (2017). *The Innovator's Dilemma*. Boston, Massachusetts: Harvard Business Review Press

Herzog, P. (2008). *Open and Closed Innovation: Different Cultures for Different Strategies*. Gabler

Sonnenberg H., Sehested C. (2011), *Lean Innovation: A Fast Path from Knowledge to Value*. Berlin, Germany. Springer-Verlag Berlin Heidelberg

Gobillot E. (2006). *The Connected Leader: Creating Agile Organisations for People, Performance and Profit*, Kogan Page

Laloux F. (2015). *Reinventing Organisations*. Brussels, Belgium. Nelson Parker

Lindberg T., Meinel C., Wagner R. (2011). *Design Thinking: Understand - Improve - Apply*. Berlin, Germany. Springer Publishing.

Schwarz, Jan Oliver (2009). *Business wargaming: Developing foresight within a strategic simulation. Technology Analysis and Strategic Management*. 21. 291-305. 10.1080/09537320902750590.

Printed in Poland
by Amazon Fulfillment
Poland Sp. z o.o., Wrocław

56015976R00081